FAMILY BUSINESS:
United We Stand–
Divided We Fall

FAMILY BUSINESS:
United We Stand—
Divided We Fall

Is Working With Relatives
Working For You?

LAURIE PICKÀRD,
M.S., N.C.C., D.A.P.A.

Avant-Courier Press

Family Business: United We Stand—Divided We Fall

For information, contact: Avant-Courier Press
A Division of: Family Business Lifestylings, L.L.C.
P.O. Box 1548
Scottsdale, AZ 85252-1548
Toll Free Phone: (877) 289-6997
Local Phone: (480) 481-6997
Fax: (480) 314-3364
e-mail: Info@familybusinesslife.com
web site: www.familybusinesslife.com

Library of Congress Catalog Card Number: 98-96610
ISBN: 0-9666978-0-4

Editing and Interior Design by:
Jennifer Ault

DEDICATION

To my beloved friend and life's partner.
I am forever grateful for your gifts:
for the time to create in surroundings
that emanate with love, encouragement, and serenity,
and for you believing in my ability to succeed
at this challenging task.
You invited me to unite with a passion
long held at bay,
creating for me the circumstances
that allowed my passage.

ACKNOWLEDGMENTS

In preparing this book for publication, I had the good fortune to be surrounded by the overwhelming generosity of people for whom I hold abundant gratitude.

To Patti Lightstone and Howard Lightstone: It was through your initial critique that I made modifications, lending improvement to my previously written words. Your combined intelligence, thoroughness, and patience were indispensable. Your generosity of time played a significant part in bringing about the success of this book, helping me to make it the best that it can be.

To Jennifer Ault: At your craft, you are gifted. Your talent appears to be limitless. Your dual role as both my copy editor and my interior design editor only proves to validate that you were my vital link. You have an "eye" for accuracy, an "ear" for language, and a "feel" for my style; all of these sensory attributes are invaluable to your trade. Your quick mind is able to articulate thoughts with fluency and ease. The care that you gave to instructing me on where to expand and improve upon my manuscript was executed with a meticulous attention to detail. Your commitment and dedication are truly appreciated.

To Glenn Pickàrd: Your unwavering readiness to help me is cherished. Your computer assistance was invaluable, from formatting my tables to inputting the corrections to my developmental editing. The dedication that you showed by arranging your work schedule in order to be available for the publishing process was most appreciated. You epitomize "partnering."

CONTENTS

Part Two: The Family's "Living-of-Business"

Part Three: Promoting Psychological and Social Wellness—Regulating Conditions of Conduct

Part Four: Becoming Developable— Working Out the Possibilities

SELF-REPORT INVENTORY

EVALUATING THE DEBITS AND CREDITS OF THE
EMOTIONAL LIFE OF YOUR BUSINESS

A Critical Analysis:

LIST OF TABLES

DISCLAIMERS

In developing my philosophy for this text, I drew upon the work of those renowned in the field of family systems theory. I take responsibility for my interpretations of the application of their theories to a family-run business. Reviewing literature on family systems theory has helped me to develop and clarify my own position. Unless I quote from a source directly, any weaving of ideas is strictly my interpretation.

This book was not written as a quick-fix program. The themes discussed here have been chosen to make one knowledgeable about matters of concern—in particular, those matters of concern that go unsaid. These themes are not presented as simple prescriptions for the complex issues that may arise in the lifestylings of a family-run business. Merely exposing the building materials—those that are defective, as well as those that are recommended but oftentimes disregarded—will of itself not be a corrective agent. This text will highlight those areas which need focused attention. You will be knowledgeable about the innate characteristics of a family-run business and, with this knowledge: (a) you will be able to determine your own primary patterns of relating, specifically those patterns which are destructive to your business; and (b) you will have the tools to stylize a well-constructed plan of renewal, designating the implementation of strategies that will serve to be advantageous to your own existing family dynamics.

Risk-worthy behaviors, while effective, inherently contain an element of risk. You must decide for yourself which risk-worthy behaviors may have too costly an outcome *for you*. Sometimes family businesses fold, and sometimes family members become estranged. There are times when this is necessary. However, you personally should never engage in any behavior in which it appears that the consequences extend beyond what you are willing to risk.

There are times in my writing in which I have used examples that are gender specific. This is for the sake of simplicity only and is in no way meant to indicate that the situations in those examples relate solely to any particular sex.

PREFACE

Family Business: United We Stand—Divided We Fall is a comprehensive study of the dual relationship that exists in all family owned and operated companies. This twofold nature of being a member in a family and then transferring that membership into employment in the family business forms an alliance that is supposedly entered into for mutual benefit. We are all familiar with the phrases "once upon a time..." and "...they all lived happily ever after." These statements have become synonymous with fairy tales. Many family-run businesses began "once upon a time" with the assumption that extending the family unit into a business setting would automatically lead to happy endings. For many, this may in fact be an enchanting but misleading belief. We have the tendency to overlook the middles of the fairy tales—the lessons. In fairy tales, there are always lessons that the main character must learn before he or she is able to come to some sort of resolution, which invariably leads to "happily ever after." In real life, however, there is not always a happy ending. The object of this book is to teach you the lessons as they are happening so that happy endings are much more likely to occur.

There is a strong connection between a family's day-to-day "business-of-living" and a family's day-to-day "living-of-business." The composition of a family's interpersonal relationship style in combination with the composition of a family's business operating procedures forms a system. This interdependent group, coming together to perform a vital function—that of growing a business—is highly influenced by the inter-relatedness of its members. The working arrangement will orient itself either toward building the bridges which will serve as pathways to guaranteeing the family-run business' future, or toward the building of walls which will serve as detriments and obstacles, preventing a secure future for the business.

This book will give you a perspective about the evolution of a family-run business' psychological and social history. It will not only capture your attention, it will also alert you to the deficiencies in your own family system and promote mindfulness as to the resulting negative consequences that you may encounter. With this knowledge, you will be in a position to accept the facts, honestly weighing the debits and credits of your family business experience.

Family members who participate in a family-run business know all too well how difficult it is at times to maintain objectivity in the workplace. The very words "family-run business" often evoke a range of emotions. For many families, purposefulness is only able to be shown through impassioned disharmony. Whether it be conflict within oneself which is unable to be appropriately expressed or conflict with others which is openly but oftentimes inappropriately expressed, the intensity of these destructive sentiments makes it difficult for the family to take pleasure from its responsibility of growing a business. These particular families (those in disharmony) are part of a fraternity. Collectively, they have not assembled. There are no enrollment fees, not even a membership roster. Yet membership dues have been paid out in conflicted emotions and/or emotional suffering.

I have written *Family Business: United We Stand—Divided We Fall* to give you, the reader, an advantage. It is healthy role behavior that sustains a functional family-run business. By accurately identifying and reflecting upon those elements of performance behavior which sabotage organizational goals, as well as a family's well-being, you have given yourself permission to be open to understanding and subsequently to defining your family's "themes." You are thus taking into account your own business relationship status. The emotional atmosphere within the company, formed through the family's style of interaction, will enhance or destroy all that is initially well-intended.

A business' very nature is to experience the process of new experiences. Typically, this includes adapting to changes in one's industry, updating operational procedures when situationally appropriate, and expanding one's customer base. Even more so, in a family-run business, experiencing the process of new experiences takes into account adapting to the expansion or alteration of roles and rules in your family, updating your perception of individual family members' capabilities, and expanding your own range of openness to participate in this professional collaborative venture. Being prepared to be open to new experiences implies being open to those changes that will accommodate (and be beneficial to) the opportunities that have the potential of bringing prosperity.

There is great inflexibility in many family-run businesses due to predetermined family roles and rules—the unspoken but implied "Thou Shalt Nots." It is imperative to identify the prevailing underlying themes which are the foundations of the various "Thou Shalt Nots" that actively impact your family's work behaviors and subsequent feelings. These themes will either have conditioned you to feel harmoniously bonded to your family's business, or you may discover the feeling that you have sentenced yourself to an indefinite term of bondage. Most relationship discomforts, most conflicted feelings, are not a result of isolated incidents. They are the result of patterns of relating that have proven to be foreseeable, based upon observations and personal experience. Being able to observe these patterns of relating makes them specific, distinct, and undeviating. Once you are able to identify the patterns and recognize when they will take effect, you can then begin to understand the dynamics of your family-run business. If left uninterrupted, these patterns of relating will continue to operate in a discomforting way without essential change.

For many, your time is now; a resocialization is in order. Practices that are intended to be mutually beneficial but are instituted through emotional reasoning are suggestive of patterns of relating that are counter-productive to organizational goals. Give yourself permission to learn to restructure your family's business life so that it is in keeping with sound professional practices—practices that are instituted through objectivity.

Much has been written about the family as a system, but traditional mental health disciplines are not by nature proficient in understanding the dynamics of a family-run business. Thus, resources have been limited. I have written this text not only to educate, but to encourage the type of growth that only comes through knowledge and introspection. While my book is written with a structure that speaks directly to the family members of a family-run business, it is also a valuable text for those who counsel, consult, and educate family-run business members. Therefore, psychotherapists, business consultants, clergy, attorneys, accountants, and business schools will find this a worthwhile addition to their libraries and classrooms as a tool to aid in understanding family-run business dynamics and to guide intervention.

On a broader scope, this text supports the premise that,

with the correct influences, if you can learn to work effectively with your relatives, then you can learn to work effectively with anybody! This goal is a true asset, as employees of an organization are a community. Like members of a family-run business, the average employee wants working conditions that are conducive to reaping non-material benefits—he or she wants to engage in productive activity for the sake of not only economic gain (working for wages), but emotional gain. Therefore, the ultimate aim of this book is to orient the reader to understanding him- or herself better. This includes how one is impacted by others, as well as how one is impacting others.

I have formatted my writing into four sections: Part One: The Family's "Business-of-Living;" Part Two: The Family's "Living-of-Business;" Part Three: Promoting Psychological and Social Wellness—Regulating Conditions of Conduct; and Part Four: Becoming Developable—Working Out the Possibilities. The chapters in each section are designed to build upon each other in order to provide an intelligent, well-rounded, thoughtful overview of those themes pertinent to a family's business dynamics. To succeed, I will have earnestly accomplished two objectives: to stimulate your mind, and to touch your heart.

Laurie Pickàrd, M.S., N.C.C., D.A.P.A.

INTRODUCTION

The Merger

The family-run business is a merger. It is the merging of the unique and varied resources that each individual in the family brings to the business. You cannot focus on the business as a separate entity if you wish to understand the dynamics of its inner workings. The group of people who comprise the family make up the business; hence, examining this makeup will help you to understand the dynamics of the business. One's emotional and intellectual process of forming opinions with regard to the private world of the family and one's outlook as to the public world of a family-run business are mutually interdependent; each relies upon the other for support. The attitudes and patterns of behavior that the family members have in relationship to each other will dominate the psychological and social well-being of the business. This point cannot be emphasized enough: *In a family-run business, the family cannot be divorced from the business.*

Psychological and Social Well-Being

The family-run business functions as a unique interactive system. It operates under two components: the business' psychological well-being, and the business' social well-being. It is not only necessary to understand the group of people who comprise the family system and how they affect and are affected by one another, but also to understand the relationship between these two inter-related components, as they will determine the stability of the family-run business over time.

Psychological well-being encompasses the thoughts and feelings that are going on within individual family members, as well as those that are exchanged between family members, as each member functions in the family-run business. These collective feelings will be reflected in the emotional overtones emanating within the system's environment. The quality of the relationship between family members takes into account their ability to be trusting and trustworthy for each other. These elements comprise a supportive environment in which one is willing to risk involvement, to self-disclose. A supportive environment provides the safety of being able to show one's professional strengths, as well as one's professional weaknesses. It also allows one to show initiative and to seek professional development, encouraging family members to reveal themselves to each other on another level—that of business associates. To be able to contribute, one cannot be held an emotional hostage by past conclusions of one's abilities, which are oftentimes misplaced. There is a need to feel confirmed, approved of, and validated. Uniting the collective individual confirmations of the family members will form a business environment which radiates psychological health. This psychological health suggests part of a family-run business' mission statement, in which members see the value of being committed to an endeavor and look forward to contributing their combined energies.

Social well-being takes into account the social contract—those patterns of behavior which are intended to be mutually beneficial. A collaborative interdependence

2

between family members fosters the business' growth through goal achievement. Therefore, one needs to negotiate the use of power and authority, exercise cooperative intentions, and define conflicts in ways that bring enrichment to the environment through constructive resolution. The business' social well-being will be determined by the family's set of values. To be professional, these values must be operational. They must be noted, in place, and adhered to through repeated and predictable behavior. To uphold the privilege and responsibility of being a participant in a family-run business means to honor and respect this "social agreement" between family members. This component of the family-run business does not just impact morale, but creates a vitality—a vitality that emanates, and thus influences, longevity.

"Accomplishment"

To accept the responsibilities of being a member of a family-run business and to take advantage of the opportunities that come from being a member, one needs more than the required business-technical skills. One needs awareness of those dynamics that will work for and against achievement of the goal of being "accomplished" as a family-run business.

The phrasing "*accomplished* family-run business" is used rather than "*successful* family-run business." This is intentional. Although they may sound as though they have the same meaning, these two words are *not* interchangeable.

Success is measured by such external standards as maintaining a relatively high profit margin, developing a wide customer base, having an adequate and on-going source of suppliers, and having a low turnover in employees.

Accomplishment exists within the private and personal interactions of a family and is influenced by relational roles—the focal point of a family-run business. This achievement of psychological and social maturity is not guaranteed by the completion of physical maturation or one's chronological age. The perception of being "accomplished" comes from a sense of true "togethering" by feeling emotionally complete, not only within oneself, but also with significant others. "Togethering" incorporates two concepts of psychological and social maturity: (a) being in possession of a healthy self-identity, in which you consciously recognize your own value; and (b) feeling that you are being recognized, validated for your selfhood, and seen as a welcomed and cherished family member. You are free to find your own balance of expressing healthy "differentness" with a blend of healthy "connectedness."

To be "successful," any business needs to function in ways that enhance its value and its merit. To be "accomplished," a family-run business has a triple task:

1. To function in enhancing ways as a business.
2. To function in enhancing ways as individuals, both within the family and within the business. This is the concept of **self-identity**.
3. To function in enhancing ways as a family, both within the family's private world and within the

family's public world. This is the concept of **connectedness**.

The degree to which one achieves this harmonious state of "accomplishment" is influenced by ingrained family dynamics. The family in harmony (working together in a healthy balance) will merge to create a work environment that is harmonious. The family in dis-ease will merge to create a work environment in dis-ease. The word "dis-ease" is distinctly different than the word "disease." The latter refers to unfavorable physical health. The former, however, indicates the social discomfort and emotional distress experienced by individuals who are confused, conflicted, and/or confined by their thoughts, feelings, and behaviors. The family that is able to overcome its emotional unrest will prosper in a work environment that has overcome a pervasive feeling of being ill-at-ease and can begin to focus its energies on growing a business.

Self-Identity

Self-identity manifests through one's individualized developmental path. It necessitates differentiation. This psychological separateness from others is a shift in focus from seeing oneself as inseparable from family to obtaining a sense that one does not have to rely upon the family for a sense of self. This developmental path is influenced by on-going interactions with family figures. To be psychologically mature, one must go through the process of being able to internalize what is in one's own best interest, a self-defining act. To be "I" before one can be "We" is imperative if, as an adult, one chooses to enter into a family-run business setting.

Family Connectedness

Connectedness is having an emotional bond born out of investing trust in another. Through that other's trustworthiness comes a feeling of safety. One is not bound by interpersonal interactions dominated by controls, dependencies, or manipulations, but rather there is an absence of coercion in choice or action that comes from the predictability of knowing that others are not operating out of a self-propelled motive, but are pure in extending themselves to be dependable, reliable, and emotionally available. This form of connectedness frees one to risk acknowledging vulnerabilities during one's professional adult development. One's journey of growth will not be used as a weapon to victimize, discredit, or shame. Gaining an internalized knowledge of self-identity, along with interpersonal competence, serves to enhance one's contribution to the family's business, and sharing these attributes in the family-run business setting can be very enriching. However, it should be noted that being "connected" in a healthy, satisfying way does not happen with good intentions alone. Families are full of well-intentioned people who are led astray.

The Lessons

The reality is that families already have their psychological and social histories. The goal by which "accomplishment" can be assessed is to personally identify the lessons that pertain to your specific family-run business situations. Give yourself permission to look beyond your financial state of affairs, which is how people often measure their societal rank—their status of prestige. Consider whether or not your family's system is in possession of stature, which is only gained from a collective psychological and social harmony—the achievement of a family growing and developing united. If this sounds like a goal rather than an actuality, there may be pitfalls that are hampering or undermining your family-run business' psychological and social well-being.

PART ONE:

THE FAMILY'S "BUSINESS OF LIVING"

CHAPTER ONE:

A FAMILY'S FUNCTION

Families have an extraordinary responsibility in the formation of their members' psychological and social maturity. I choose the word "extraordinary" because it implies an "extra-ordinary" responsibility that surpasses the usual privileges accorded someone with a distinct official position of having power and authority over a group of people. *Nothing* exceeds a family in the scale-of-quality or degree-of-importance for influencing both identity formation and the extent to which one is emotionally complete in his or her ability to form and maintain pleasurable relationships. Both are characteristics associated with how one's personality is expressed and the state of one's mental health. By nature of being titled "family," authority figures are elevated to a prestigious position that extends their range of limits beyond that accorded any other caretaker.

Virginia Satir (1972) states, "The family is the factory where a person is made. The adults are the peoplemakers" (p.3). These "peoplemakers" are shapers, molding the experiences of those entrusted in their care, building one experience upon another. In its totality, this influences the process of forming—of "growing"—an individual. Since one's actions as an adult parental figure will ultimately form a human-being, one needs to ask: What skills am I equipped with to carry out this function? After all, a dependent child does not have the privilege of demanding stipulations that equate with "fulfillment" in this parent-child contract. So, too, not all adult parental figures come with the same standard equipment.

Adult parental figures generally do not come into this extra-ordinary responsibility with the intent to deprive their children of the emotional nurturing and psychological support that they need to become healthy adults. Some take on this responsibility well-informed—educated as to having some awareness of anticipated consequences of their forthcoming actions. Some have a natural ability to parent. Some enter into this relationship with blind faith. Far too many parental figures are in possession of and utilize defective skills. Just as fingerprints leave a patterned impression as to one's identification, one's care-giving style leaves a patterned impression upon the personality and mental health of the human-being that one is parenting.

Rules of conduct are believed to be the underlying ingredients that characterize the comprehensive obligation of molding the psychology of a human-being. Through applying rules of conduct, one can opt to form a "family system" whereby: (a) one is encouraged and free to move toward identity formation, known as differentiation, *and* one is able to bond by forming healthy attachments with adult parental figures; or (b) one is discouraged and hindered in his or her movement toward differentiation, *and* one's emotional bonding is disordered, resulting from mental or emotional stress or injury. These two dynamics of differentiation and emotional bonding are distinct aspects of personality development which operate simultaneously. The aftereffects of what happens during a person's developmental stages may leave him or her (as a member in a "family system") without "a secure base" for "protection, comfort, and support" (Bowlby, 1988, p.121). Without this, one is left feeling deprived and cheated out of a genuine sense of belonging.

Differentiation is having a relationship with oneself, a self that possesses characteristics that distinguish the individual from the whole ("whole" implying the family). In a healthily functioning family, one is encouraged to develop different characteristics, to be distinct in personhood, to be emotionally mature. Murray Bowen (1994), in his writings of Family Systems Theory, wrote that the differentiation of self has two poles: the "solid-self" (or "basic self") and the "pseudo-self" (or "pretend self").

The "solid-self," Bowen writes, "is made up of clearly defined beliefs, opinions, convictions and life principles" (p.365). "The basic self may be changed from within self on the basis of new knowledge and experience. The basic self is *not negotiable in the relationship system*; in that it is not changed by coercion or pressure, or to gain approval, or enhance one's stand with others" (p.473). Therefore, the solid-self, due to intellectual awareness (versus one's emotions ruling), "joins or rejects membership [in the group]...based on careful weighing of the advantages and

13

disadvantages.... The solid-self says 'This is who I am, what I believe, what I stand for, and what I will do and will not do,' in any given situation" (p.365).

The "pseudo-self," Bowen writes, will "lose self to the other [since the] pseudo-self is created by emotional pressure...because it is required or considered right by the group" (p.365). Therefore, "the greater the emotional fusion into a common self with others...the greater the degree of undifferentiation." This pseudo-self, this undifferentiated self, can equate to a "no self" (p.472).

Forming attachments within the family unit, and specifically with one's parental figures, influences the shaping of an individual's personality. Providing one with "a secure base" within the family unit gives one the confidence to step outside of the convictions of the family and thereby actively build the solid-self. This, then, gives one the freedom to explore one's environment (Bowlby, 1988, p.121). This exploration entails the degree to which and the style of how one will risk involvement in relationships. Similarly, one's attachment style reflects one's feelings of self-worth and self-confidence. These attempts at seeking love, approval, and attention will ultimately influence one's strategy for coping with anxiety, how vulnerable one will be to stress, and one's expectations of self, others, and life itself (Bowlby, 1988, pp.119-125). Ryan and Lynch (1989) note that it is "attachment" to parents, and not the feeling of emotional detachment from one's parents, that enhances individuation (differentiation) in adolescence and early adulthood. This is usually the crucial time frame in which one develops career interests and makes career choices, ultimately influencing that person's emotional agenda—the reasonings behind why he or she will (or will not) become involved in the family-run business.

From the works of Bowen, Bowlby, and Ryan and Lynch,

it becomes relevant to consider how relationship difficulties in a family-run business are inter-related with family members' past attachment history and, thus, the different degrees of differentiation upon entering a family-run business. To be functioning as a professional in a professional work environment, and particularly in a family-run business, one is best served by being able to observe and function outside of the emotional field of the family. Business decisions are to be objective and intellectually based, not subjective and emotionally ruled. One element that is necessary for attaining and maintaining psychological and social well-being is for a family-run business to be **time competent**—to function in the here-and-now and yet effectively intertwine the family's and the family-run business' past with visions and goals for its future. Given these considerations, you must determine which family relationship dynamics are and are not changeable.

CHAPTER TWO:

A FAMILY'S EMOTIONAL SYSTEM

Open Relationship Configuration
versus
Closed Relationship Configuration

A family is a set of relationships operating under an emotional system. The adult parental figures have the option of exercising power and authority over this group of people to create an emotional system that is "open" (emotionally receptive) in its relationship configuration. Or they can create an emotional system that is "closed" (emotionally cut off) in its relationship configuration. The word "configuration," in this context, denotes the family members (each member being a part of the emotional system) as having been arranged to function in a particular way, to "co"-operate. Bowen writes, "There are wide variations in the frequency and quality of relationships in cut-offs and in openness" (1994, p.537).

In an open or emotionally receptive relationship configuration, family members are invited to embrace the journey of working toward individuation, not to fear it. In a closed or emotionally cut off relationship configuration, taking on the responsibility of defining oneself as separate from the family is an intimidating task, as it signifies a risk of challenging the rules of the family system. In a closed relationship environment, rules cannot be challenged or altered, even when it is appropriate to do so. In challenging the rules, one is confronting one's own interpersonal and social fears—fear of rejection, fear of failure, fear of loss, as well as fear of closeness. In a closed relationship configuration, working toward individuation is limited and controlled, often punishable. There are repercussions when one challenges or tries to grow beyond the rigid, inflexible boundaries of this closed system. Members who are discouraged from thinking for themselves, who abdicate this developmental task of individuation, become emotionally cut off from a relationship with themselves.

Working toward individuation is a journey, not an event—an intended life's walk. As one's definition of "self" evolves, one may redefine one's relationships with significant others. In a closed relationship configuration, this is interpreted as competing with the family's emotional system, and thus, individuation becomes a threat to the family. This is why, in a closed relationship configuration, working toward individuation, which leads to differentiation (a defining of self), is discouraged by adult parental figures and hampered by control, manipulation, and dependency.

As a result, one learns during childhood to shut down and deny the desire and the need to self-define. This is the time when one's interpersonal and social fears are formed. It is during adulthood that one brings these fears into the family business. One may desire initiating expanding the parameters of his or her assigned job description, or one may recognize the need to enhance or institute operational procedures. However, there is a direct correlation between obediently not challenging the family's emotional system and how this obedience carries over into one's family business relationship status. This will be in evidence in one's identifiable, individual performance style and how one copes with his or her internalized conflict. One may desire to engage in risk-worthy behavior that could not only raise one's mastery over his or her professional world, but ultimately legitimize and thus validate one as an adult. This desire has to co-exist with the diametrically opposed anticipatory anxiety at the thought of being censured or criticized for wanting to grow and to be validated as an adult. In the end, the desire to "play-it-safe" may lead to a perpetual dis-ease at maintaining the status quo.

Without the freedom to explore, experience, risk expression of, and develop a true self-identity (a "solid-self" versus a "pseudo-self"), what emerges is a "you" who has learned to adapt in an attempt to feel some small, meaningful sense of emotional connectedness. Virginia Satir (1972) states simply, "Your self-worth, your communication, together with your rules and your beliefs are the ingredients that make up your family system" (p.118). It is with these ingredients in mind that one needs to define a family's emotional system. An emotional system that is not a static structure is one that is flexible and evolving and has a blending of both closeness (healthy attachment) and separateness (differentiation) in which both are seen as accessible.

It's like owning a pair of shoes that look nice, but feel as though they don't fit quite right. To find an excuse to hold onto the shoes and to keep them in your possession, you tell yourself that you'll make do. You talk yourself into adjusting to the discomfort. But the discomfort is always there; sometimes it is more pronounced than at other times. Ultimately, this takes its toll on your ability to walk distance or to be on your feet for long periods of time. You adapt to the confinement, the restrictiveness, despite the unrelenting dis-ease you feel in your feet. Your resistance to change to alternative shoes has over time impaired far more than your way of thinking; it has also damaged your feet. A shoe metaphor seems especially appropriate, since shoes are meant to support and cushion you as you transport yourself in life's daily walk. If you set out with a pair of shoes that do not fit, you feel the stress of the journey heightened and you can find reasons to turn back, sabotaging the pleasure of achieving completion at your journey's end.

In this metaphor, one learns a distorted lesson of life: that one is not to thrive, only to make-do; that to be acceptable, one must live as a "pseudo-self"—to look as if all is "nice" on the outside, even though internal discomfort indicates that all is not "quite right." One also learns to sacrifice oneself if one wants to be associated with one's family; that membership is conditional and restrictive, just as ill-fitting shoes are restrictive.

Webster's dictionary states that if something is closed, it implies that it had in some way been open, or perhaps unfinished. Pertaining to a closed relationship configuration, this suggests that alternatives are recognized and, though enticing, are a threat. Somewhere the meanings of "connectedness" and "self-identity" have become misunderstood. Genuine interpersonal connect-edness, as well as self-identity, implies a freedom of movement, a distinction between an individual as a family member and the individual as "self." Parental figures who impose their own fears upon the innocent do not intend to confine or to restrict freedom of expression. These individuals, while in a position of authority, merely demonstrate behaviors as a formula to cope with their own real or imagined threats.

Table 1 lists familiar phrases symbolic of family relationships—those characteristics that are indicative of both open and closed family configurations.

Table 1:
FAMILIAR PHRASES SYMBOLIC OF FAMILY RELATIONSHIPS

Open Family Configuration	Closed Family Configuration
OPEN-MINDED • Receptive to ideas • Willing to listen and hear, so as to be able to consider, accept, and deal with matters needing to be addressed • Exposed to knowledge	**CLOSED-MINDED** • Behavior is confined to a restricted level • Desire for the system to maintain itself without threat from the outside • Self-contained; no additions
OPEN-DOOR • Freedom to allow passage; no confining barrier • Going beyond the initial restrictions to growth, life's passage • Not repressed by controls, regulations, or restraints • Able to convert the understanding of aftereffects to constructive problem-solving	**CLOSED-DOOR** • Strict rules • Rigid in attitude • Closed to negotiation • Little space for freedom of expression beyond the restrictions imposed by the system • Secretive; needs, feelings, and thoughts cannot be expressed verbally with confidence and ease
OPEN-POSITIONED • Not rigidly fixed • Available to possibilities or to opportunities unfolding • Clearing away obstructions to make pathways useable and visible	**CLOSED-POSITIONED** • Ignore deliberately • Exclude outside influence • Deny any view of alternatives
OPEN-HEARTED • Receptive to emotional appeal • Perceiving vulnerabilities of others without taking them on as your own	**CLOSED-HEARTED** • Uncaring; feelings appear frozen • Insensitive disregard for the welfare of others; inhuman

CHAPTER THREE

FOOD FOR THOUGHT

By now, you most likely realize that a family with a closed relationship configuration who has invested in the formation of and participation in a family-run business has borrowed against this privilege and will come out short. *There will be unintended negative consequences.*

As change cannot occur without insight, let us go further in assessing the different aspects that comprise a family's emotional system: self-worth, communication, rules, and beliefs. This grouping of items makes up the emotional system in much the same way that a recipe is made up of different ingredients.

Families are reported to "thrive" on tradition. As such,

one of the ways that families perpetuate this time-honored demonstration is through stimulating the senses via food—preparing traditional recipes and gathering to partake of the benefits of this meal. A traditional recipe is one that is passed down from generation to generation. Families come to rely upon these smells and tastes and sights for a sense of well-being. The recipe-maker's intent is to make a nurturing contribution to the family table. Yet, preparation is automatic, robotic, and lacking conscious thought as to the true nutritional value of the ingredients. One ingests with little regard as to what one is actually ingesting. Portions are not monitored; the more that is ingested, the more the recipe-maker feels that his or her efforts are appreciated. For some, changing one ingredient is seen as sacrilegious. Those who do recognize that what is being ingested may not, in fact, be healthy eat anyway, even if it gives physical discomfort, because they don't want to offend. And so the tradition continues.

The open system family appreciates the traditional as much as the closed system family does, but it also recognizes the need and the desire for a more nutritionally fulfilling value. Its members want food for the soul. So they take a "tried and true" recipe, passed from generation to generation, and they feel encouraged to risk altering the ingredients. There are no unrealistic expectations that the taste and texture be exactly the same, for an alternative naturally suggests change. The recipe-maker in both the open system family and the closed system family is well-intentioned; he or she has made an investment in ingredients and in preparation time. However, the outcomes for the two are radically different.

Food is intended to nourish—to provide energy, to promote growth, and to sustain life. With this "food for thought," ask yourself these questions: If a closed system family will only partake of traditional recipes, and the recipe-maker's intent is to provide an enrichment to a family gathering, then why do so many have physical ailments in anticipation of or following the meal? And why, in spite of these ailments, do these individuals continue to ingest the recipes?

Just as ingesting food that is not life-sustaining represents a resistance to nurturing your physical health, continuing to ingest outdated rules that limit your patterns of relating represents a resistance to nurturing your emotional health. Barriers are erected. Possibilities appear limited. The unknown is feared. You need to give permission to yourself to create a mentality in which you learn to trust the process of life.

As this metaphor of the "traditional recipe" advocates, adjusting ingredients to enhance your family's emotional system is a worthwhile endeavor. You do possess the capability to eliminate that which causes negative consequences. Attempting to resist, distrust, or outsmart the process of life is no longer a substantial option. There comes a point when a vital decision must be made—breaking up or breaking through.

Neither breaking up nor breaking through guarantees resolution. Yet both require action intended to be beneficial as a means of dealing with on-going difficulties—to free yourself from emotional restraints, to remove restrictive conditions. Both are intended to establish and restore favorable circumstances in order for your family to operate in an unimpaired condition. However, breaking up could imply that your family will only maintain its former condition, just no longer conducting these maladaptive behaviors in a work setting. Breaking up occurs *because of* difficulties, obstacles, or discouragement. Breaking through is a form of perseverance. It is taking an unyielding course of action *in spite of* difficulties, obstacles, or discouragement. Breaking through takes determination and is in evidence when issues are directly addressed, resistance is eliminated, and fear of the unknown is in abeyance.

Individual family members may need to go their separate ways; your business may choose to fold; your family may remain divided. So, too, the opportunity to unearth collaborative potential will go unexplored. You decide which direction is more valued: breaking up or breaking through. *It is your choice.*

CHAPTER FOUR:

RECIPE INGREDIENT FOR A FAMILY'S EMOTIONAL SYSTEM– SELF-WORTH

> - **Self-Worth**
> - Communication
> - Rules
> - Beliefs

"I always seem to be feeling either superior or inferior, one up or one down, better off or worse off than anyone else. The superior moments are when I feel equal."

Hugh Prather

This quote from *Notes to Myself: My Struggle to Become a Person* (1970) is not meant to imply that everyone in a family is a social equal. A parent who has been working in business and raising a child is not by role definition a social equal with that child. Nor is one who has been in business for years a professional equal with one who is a novice. Many equate equality with uniformity, but equality merely means that people, despite their individual differences and abilities, have equal claim to dignity and respect. This is not an entitlement, but a privilege that is earned by nature of being a person who lives life engaged in behaviors that are worthy. Recognition is then deservedly acquired through commendable acts.

When one comes from a closed relationship con-figuration, one feels dis-eased by one's interpersonal relationships, particularly those with adult parental figures. One comes to believe that one lacks the ability to cope with those things that happen as a natural flow of life. Consequently, one feels inferior and does not strive to claim dignity and respect. In low self-esteem thinking, one does not possess the courage to be imperfect, to risk making mistakes, and to fail at a new "self-defining" task without feeling lowered in one's own self-worth. Being discouraged then becomes inevitable; one comes to believe that feeling unfinished and incomplete will be forever-lasting. Having a lack of faith in one's ability to succeed at being self-sufficient, as well as not having found one's healthy, distinct place in the family, are not only sources of discouragement, but they could paralyze one's willingness to make risk-worthy choices that might ultimately empower.

The beliefs that one carries about oneself as a person have a tendency to influence the way one chooses to interact with others in the family, as well as in the family-run business environment. If one sees oneself as situationally inadequate when comparing oneself to others, the subsequent fear is that others will permanently see one as developmentally inadequate and will unceasingly shame him or her for it.

Rudolf Dreikurs (1964) writes, "We cannot protect our

children from life. Therefore, it is essential to prepare them for it.... Parental love is best demonstrated through constant encouragement towards independence" (pp.51-55).

The closed relationship configuration is designed to minimize and/or deter the contamination of outside influences which would support and encourage involvement toward "independence." In trying to overcome real or imagined threats, the closed relationship configuration's power and authority figures begin to "over-protect" or "over-control." All of this increases rather than decreases one's anxiety. While effective in the short run for removing one's consideration for working toward individuation, in the long run, a closed relationship configuration will experience negative consequences.

While people recognize the value of self-worth and want recognition that is positively influenced and earned, there is the tendency to compromise that which they value. This sets them up for further feelings of inadequacy and further self-neglect. **Self-neglect** (in this context) is characterized by a careless indifference to the establishment of educational, vocational, or avocational goals, and being inattentive to the discipline needed to fulfill said goals. Overall, it is an unfaithfulness to oneself by not making an attempt to achieve self-defined success. Although self-sabotaging, it becomes enticing to follow a path of success that is other-defined. **Other-defined success** is described as an authority figure's use of power (either through another's obedience or through emulation) to impose predetermined, oftentimes ill-conceived and unrealistic, expectations onto someone else of what that person *should* aspire to achieve.

When someone chooses to predetermine and measure another's success, it tends to originate with a bias. This one-sided predisposition is generally prompted by the enticing prospect of being influential in another's developmental task of establishing and achieving life goals. The eager and enthusiastic use of one's position to lure another is a seductive behavior, as the one doing the luring is oftentimes motivated by the need to either: (a) compensate for one's own life goals going unfulfilled, thus achieving satisfaction through vicariously living out one's dreams of success through another; or (b) depend upon another to achieve a self-defined goal that cannot be fulfilled solely by one's own interests, skills, or energies.

The individual who is being lured may be unsuspecting of the lure-ee's motivations; however, with or without this understanding, the lure is tempting. In choosing to be other-directed, the low self-esteem thinker generally pursues a path that is least challenging, a path that is readily available, or a path that appears to hold the most promise for fulfilling one's yearning for recognition. On the one hand, the low self-esteem thinker becomes reconciled to self-imposed limitations; on the other hand, this encourages discontent. To compensate for the internalized conflict over the recognition of self-neglect and the accompanying fears and anxiety, an art form of pretending follows. This is when we create a "pseudo-self." The correlation to family is this: the more dis-eased one interprets the family's emotional system to be, the more elaborate the facade; the family member creates a concealing mask to shield him or her from possible humiliation and despair.

This facade (one's attempt at hiding one's feelings of inadequacy), while self-protective in nature, works against differentiation. Recognition is obtained through indirect communication and by setting others up to react to you in the ways that you want them to react. In actuality, this is a process of manipulation, which then acts as a vehicle to achieving power and influence over others. It is motivated by fear and by unrealistic expectations. Seeing oneself through a lens of fear, one victimizes oneself with one's own expectations. This "what if...then..." syndrome is counterproductive to establishing a cohesive family-run business environment.

You are what you are committed to. If you are committed to being a low self-worth family member in a family-run business environment, then you will:

- Expect to be stepped on.
- Expect to be treated disrespectfully.
- Expect to doubt yourself and subsequently to give up control.
- Expect difficulty in carrying out your job.
- Expect to be exposed as someone who is ill-equipped to perform your job description.
- Expect others to be closed to your opinions.
- Expect yourself to lack clarity of thought.
- Expect lack of cooperation.
- Expect to feel emotionally isolated instead of part of a team.
- Expect others to be insensitive to your feelings.

How, then, do you make yourself known to others without needing to set them up to react in the ways that you want or without wearing a facade to hide your perceived inadequacy? John Powell, in his book *Why am I Afraid to Tell You Who I Am?* (1969), writes, "I am afraid to tell you who I am, because, if I tell you who I am, you may not like who I am, and it's all that I have" (p.12). Reflecting back to the concept of self-identity and the process of togethering, it was noted that to be "accomplished," a family-run business has a triple task: (a) to function in ways that

31

enhance the business; (b) to function in ways that enhance one as an individual, both within the family and within the business (self-identity); and (c) to function in ways that enhance the family, both within the family's private world and within the family's public world (connectedness). If a family member feels inadequate and, in the private world of family, believes that this has been reinforced, then how does this person enter a family-run business without fear and expectations of doom? The self-evaluative message is: "All that I have is not enough."

Whenever you carry this belief of "all that I have is not enough," you hypnotize yourself into believing that you are less capable than you really are. You carry an unrealistic appraisal of yourself and your abilities to cope with whatever life brings you. Consequently, the games, the maneuvers to protect yourself from further anticipated hurt, humiliation, and despair, undermine not only yourself, but the family-run business as well.

As Rudolf Dreikurs (1964) simply and insightfully notes, "A bruised knee will mend: bruised courage may last a lifetime" (p.42).

CHAPTER FIVE:

RECIPE INGREDIENT FOR A FAMILY'S EMOTIONAL SYSTEM— COMMUNICATION

> - Self-Worth
> - **Communication**
> - Rules
> - Beliefs

You are the Product: Stylizing the Individual

The greatest fear typically associated with the belief of "all that I have is not enough" is that when you enter the world of business, YOU are the product that is being sold. Alfred Adler (1912) believed that the "basic dynamic force" of personality structure is a "striving for superiority," not as a marker of contrast of the individual within a group or as a position of power, but as a method "for overcoming... for completion... for self-enhancement... a movement [directing one] from one point to another" (cited in Ansbacher, H. L., & Ansbacher, R. R., 1964, p.13). However, this psychological need to be fulfilled by one's potentialities is not enough; there is also the social need for validation, which Eric Berne coined "recognition hunger" (1964, p.15). This **recognition hunger**, according to Berne, is an individual's psychological need for approval, a striving for social meaning.

Establishing power with a style of command that will produce the desired effect of influencing a family's workplace requires persuasion, specifically if it is for one's own personal gain. This creates a unique and significant form of anxiety when one needs to use persuasion on those who have had years of forming opinions of him or her. Recognizing, possibly on some covert level, that one will never fully achieve a sense of *completion* escalates the already existing tension that comes with self-dissatisfaction. **Completion** is defined as a state of fulfillment and closure, as one has aspired and obtained all that one desires, both within one's reach and possibly beyond one's reach.

How, then, do you get "recognized" for working toward fulfilling your potential when you make a lateral move from your family's at-home closed relationship configuration into your family's work environment with the belief that "all that I am is not enough?" *Again, you carry this feeling of inadequacy, built upon your subjective interpretation of your psychological and social disabilities, from a perception of self which has been developed from your interactions with others.*

Thus, you adapt. You try to *maneuver* and out-maneuver those whom you need to persuade. Persuasion is your vehicle for obtaining power and influence. Your choice of *tactics* will depend upon your perceived position of power, your expectations of how others will react to you, what you set out to accomplish, and what has worked for you with family members in the past. Given that a closed relationship configuration does not communicate openly, directly, honestly, and with flexibility for cooperative intentions, your task becomes complicated. To perform in "self-oriented" ways, a *defense route* is needed in order to achieve some form of recognition. Keep in mind that if you carry low self-esteem thinking, you believe that your happiness is in another's hands. You want to be self-developed, but with low self-esteem thinking ("I am inferior." "I am inadequate." "I am not enough."), your recognition hunger has you convinced that self-development will only come through being validated by others—others who historically have proven themselves difficult to please unless you comply with their rules and beliefs. You start to believe, "I would only be happy if he/she would...."

If you already carry past experiences coated with discouragement, you will naturally assume that others' opinions of your work will be negative. You are preparing your *persuasion strategies* with anticipation and a state of mind that may be inappropriate, given the reality of the facts. In an all-consuming desire to fill your hunger for recognition, you become stuck developmentally. In being led by your emotions rather than by facts and experiences, you become off-balance. Fulfilling a greater developmental need—that of achieving your different-ness (differentiation), a sense of your own self-worth, and a striving for completion—is left unattended and denied.

You need to give yourself permission to dispel irrational beliefs. The following statements are precursors to eliminating unwarranted and troubling negative self-talk.

- I am not inadequate; I have only been programmed to believe so.
- I am deluding myself if I believe that I will receive the recognition I seek if I just comply with the restrictive rules and beliefs of others.
- I will be investing my time and my emotional energy to no avail if I continue to disregard what has historically shown itself to be true.
- I can no longer sacrifice my differentness by adhering to the unrealistic expectations of others.

A defective cognitive-emotional system is one that lacks clarity in awareness and judgment, with particular susceptibility to excessive sensitiveness in feelings. When you are prone to be easily offended or emotionally hurt, you have a tendency to engage in the act of overemphasizing the meanings of facts in a given situation. This faulty reasoning is labeled **exaggeration**. Likewise, you are also inclined to evaluate and relabel facts so that your interpretation of them is disproportionate to the reality of the situation. This faulty reasoning is labeled **distortion**. Both exaggeration and distortion are based on an emotional, rather than on a rational, process. This is a byproduct of adapting and molding to a surrounding culture that has stifled self-enhancement and denounced your psychological need for approval. Your response becomes one in which you assume, on some level, that you will once again feel discouraged when the approval that you are seeking is withheld. This emotionality not only affects self-worth, but it also undermines your strength of character when vitality of spirit is needed to cope with the conflicting challenges of life.

MANEUVERS. TACTICS. DEFENSES. STRATEGIES. All of these are words which sound like preparation for "war games." Yet, are you not at war within yourself? In this internalized war, this inner-conflict, you arm yourself with a defense strategy that fits within your own realm of comfort.

Thus, you develop your influence style, your "game plan." If you are in an open relationship configuration, you will have influence styles that are colleague-based, displaying cooperative intentions that are business focused. There is no need for tactics or defense strategies when you believe, "I am enough." You feel that your movement toward fulfilling your potential is being validated from within and from others. You have a self-identity that is genuine, not a facade built upon a need to self-protect. *You do not see yourself lacking.* If you are in a closed relationship configuration, you will have influence styles that are power-based, displaying a performance style that is self-focused with the goal of having an advantage over others. One system operates primarily in harmony, the other system in on-going conflict—conflict that is internalized and/or with others. One chosen performance style leaves a family struggling just to be "a team;" the other paves the way toward a family becoming "The A-Team," The Accomplished Team.

Remember the television show *The A-Team*? The characters in that show comprised a team of individuals, each possessing uniquely differentiated talents which, when used interdependently, achieved a togethering that was undefeatable regardless of the obstacles put in their way. In a crisis, they thrived due to the cooperative intentions for the psychological and social well-being of all. Their adversaries always lost because they were always self-focused, needing to overpower others through manipulation. *The A-Team* was an example of "The Accomplished Team": they loved, supported, and

37

encouraged each other like a family; they stood united, not divided; they stood where others had fallen.

Individual Performance Styles

Let us now continue by looking at those individual performance styles that are representative of a family that is internally divided. Keep in mind the following six points:

1. Power and influence styles for a closed relationship configuration focus on promoting "self-interest," not the team's best interest.
2. Power and influence styles are one's attempt to compensate for feelings of inadequacy.
3. The differences between people are evidenced by their chosen styles of performance.
4. No particular performance style is static. Performers can fluctuate in their choice of roles, or they can blend roles, depending upon who they are trying to influence. It is true, however, that people do tend to show preferences in their functioning styles.
5. Individuals who are members of a family that is internally divided demonstrate a self-protective strategy when feeling psychologically unsafe in the family work environment. These strategies are manifested in performance styles that can be labeled as signs of resistance. Resistance can also be interpreted as a control issue, since feeling emotionally endangered provokes a protective response—to avoid feeling powerless.
6. Resistance is an internalized code to indicate potential peril—one's personal distress call.

To respond with resistance is empowering. In its dominant state, this avenue for seeking power, while protecting oneself from feeling psychologically endangered, also deprives one of optimism and enthusiasm, as well as discourages compliance. In this regard, resistance is provocative, as it thwarts cooperation. This state of unrest is unsuitable to the demands of the work environment, since it covers up feelings, stirs up disagreement, gives rise to anger, produces opposition, and creates impasses. Thus, resistance holds promise to a secondary gain—an unconscious wish to avoid change. As a form of avoidance, resistance impedes interdependence, preserves the dysfunction of the family system, and maintains the status quo.

The following 12 influence styles are broken down into degrees under the headings of two basic categories: **The Conformists** and **The Oppositionists**. When one is a conformist, one may be apathetic, submissive, obedient, or compliant. When one is an oppositionist, one is motivated to violate, to antagonize, and to combat, stimulating different degrees of emotion as the aggressiveness of the action heightens. Both categories are provocative in that they influence by arousing feelings or actions in others. All 12 styles hinder team development in varying degrees by presenting a difficulty in interpersonal communication.

Table 2:
PICKÀRD'S INDIVIDUAL PERFORMANCE STYLES: "THE CONFORMISTS"

SELF-ALIENATED PERFORMER
- Won't take responsibility
- Does not problem-solve in own area; lacks initiative
- Will not make decisions; "It's up to you."
- No assimilation into business culture
- Withholds any efforts or contributions that would serve to influence the outcome of business

SELF-SERVING PERFORMER
- Enlists sympathy from others
- Presents self as a victim
- Acts as though always under pressure
- Attempts to provoke guilt in others if others expect productivity
- Work may be neglected or of inferior quality

SELF-RESTRICTED PERFORMER
- Forces others to direct in what needs to be done next
- Work done is inferior in quality; "why bother" attitude
- Presents an appearance without substance
- Appears to be lacking in depth of knowledge
- Keeps self in the background; reserved

SELF-JUSTIFYING PERFORMER
- Appears reassuring and supportive
- Amiable disposition; causes no resistance
- Works to avoid disagreeable outcomes; smooth-tongued
- May pretend to be unaware of environmental dis-ease in order to achieve a degree of satisfaction to justify oneself by not "making waves" and by people-pleasing

Table 2:
PICKÀRD'S INDIVIDUAL PERFORMANCE STYLES: "THE CONFORMISTS," cont'd.

SELF-SACRIFICING PERFORMER
- Acts to save, free, or rescue others from destruction, calamity, or danger
- Tries to free others from the negative consequences of their choices
- Appears to have no concern for self; self-less actions
- Behavior believed to be useful or valuable, but enables the one being "saved" to not take responsibility for self
- Has problems saying no; gullible

SELF-SOOTHING PERFORMER
- Self-protective strategy used when experiencing "overload"
- Capable and hard-working, but feels temporarily overloaded with work; "Enough is enough." "Give me a break already."
- Becomes physically sick when working under pressure for extended periods of time
- Extreme stress manifests in physical illness—a vehicle to justify feeling a need for relief

SELF-IMPORTANT PERFORMER
- Exaggerates notion of own importance
- Works above and beyond the standard expected level
- May provoke in others admiration or jealousy for achievements
- Self-sacrificing; appears to be company-oriented

Table 3:
PICKÀRD'S INDIVIDUAL PERFORMANCE STYLES: "THE OPPOSITIONISTS"

SELF-CONCEITED PERFORMER
- "My way" oriented, which is not always in the best interest of the company; doing own thing by own rules
- Closed to the input of others, disregarding good advice and the realities of a situation; "It's their problem, not mine."
- Human-beings come second, the task of "my way" comes first; makes others feel incompetent or helpless
- Glosses over own mistakes and weaknesses; exaggerates own good qualities and achievements
- Inflexible; argumentative

SELF-DEALING PERFORMER
- Takes from others primarily for own advantage
- Intrudes into others' areas of responsibility, not for "mutual" advantage
- Shows unrestraint in thrusting oneself into the affairs of others, with fighting disposition, if necessary
- Unprovoked, violates the boundaries of others

SELF-OBSCURING PERFORMER
- Conceals own inadequacies in knowledge, exhibited by deliberate undermining of another's professional standing with the goal of defeating and making others feel inferior
- Provokes feelings of inadequacy in others with intent to cause deterioration in mind and performance
- Decreases the endurance of others, resulting in weariness or impatience of spirit
- Overpowers others with discourteous or annoying behavior, causing others to feel displeasure with self and work

Table 3:
PICKÀRD'S INDIVIDUAL PERFORMANCE STYLES: "THE OPPOSITIONISTS," cont'd.

SELF-COMPELLING PERFORMER
- Demands attention by presenting an air of superiority with the goal to intimidate
- Places overwhelming pressure on others, causing others to be timid and/or fearful
- Shows discourteous and offensive behavior with intent to frighten
- Inflames anger in others by exhibiting overbearing conduct; aim is to intensify feelings of inferiority in others

SELF-DESTRUCTING PERFORMER
- Engages in destructive behavior, endangering self as well as bringing possible harm to others and the family-run business
- Unmanageable; out-of-control
- Resists intervention or self-management
- Defiant

People in general carry unrealistic expectations about their relationships. In particular is the distorted belief that others can mind-read our intentions, that one should be able to understand another without verbally sharing feelings or thoughts. One wants to be able to have one's emotional curtains drawn and yet expects that another should instinctively comprehend when he or she needs to feel close and when he or she needs distance. One believes that others should be able to correctly read nonverbal cues without anyone expressing a word.

In a closed relationship configuration, healthy connectedness is lacking and genuine closeness is limited. This may be in evidence through a situation-specific event. Or it may be reflected in your internal rules of conduct, whereby you share only part of yourself and with only a few. Then, too, it may be because you have created a false closeness, in which you present a facade and then deceive yourself that you have achieved connectedness. In any case, unrealistic expectations and feelings of emotional distance with those who are labeled as "significant others" cause an emptiness within.

Thomas Fogarty (1996) looked at emotional states of "inner emptiness" which are caused by "the realization of the limitations of what individuals could expect to get from their relationships" (p.17). Expanding on this theory, inner emptiness collectively comes from Fogarty's perspective, Berne's theory on recognition hunger, and a third element. This third element takes into consideration the self-protective behavioral and attitudinal restrictions that one imposes upon oneself with intent to regulate ongoing inner-conflict and the resulting emotional discomfort. It is this collective viewpoint that shapes the way in which one imposes one's style of influence over another, thereby preventing the forming or maintaining of genuine closeness—thus, one is left feeling an emptiness within.

As depicted in Pickàrd's 12 Individual Performance Styles, a self-interest performance level sabotages and undermines business-interest performance and team development. While one's performance style is an internalized decision to compensate for the feeling that one has not mastered one's environment, such behavior is doubly purposeful, since it also sends messages to a second party. The second party will interpret the message-sender's style and determine whether he or she can be in the "power position," exercising power through control, manipulation, and the fostering of dependency. This control is held by a non-verbal agreement, an unspoken pact as to who will further sacrifice him- or herself for the one who will be "on top." This promotes another destructive dynamic, which is portrayed in the dyad. A **dyad** consists of two parts, and used in a social context, refers to two persons involved in an ongoing relationship or interaction.

The Dyad Relationship: Dynamics of Power Positioning

Alfred Adler's (1912) "interpersonal, social theory of personality" takes into account both "healthy development and deviations in terms of relationships" (cited in Ansbacher, H. L. & Ansbacher, R. R., 1964, p.382). Adler believed that when one recognizes that one's expectations of others are not being met, the way in which one tries to meet one's perceived needs of fulfilling one's inner emptiness is by either constructive means (healthy development) or destructive means (deviations). This choice of action is influenced by the desire to attract attention and will manifest either in a style of cooperation or in a style of competitiveness and jealousy toward others.

When one is engaged in a closed family-run business configuration, the power position in a dyad will go to the one whose influence style manifests itself in one of Pickàrd's three Relationship Control Styles: The Restrictive Relationship; The Demanding Relationship; or The Oppressive Relationship. The psychological payoff for the individual who adopts any one of these three control styles as his or her line of defense is that it gives an illusion of security. The balance between emotional closeness and emotional distance—one's comfort level—is perceived to be under one's control. One cannot risk exposing one's own fear of "all that I have is not enough." Consequently, the focus is on gaining power over others. This power is achieved by controlling emotions and behavior—either by being dependent upon others, or by creating dependency in others.

Achieving power by being dependent upon others is characterized by regularly engaging in behavior that is destructive, irresponsible, inappropriate, or unhealthy. In regard to this text, this behavior is not only detrimental to the one whose actions are improper, but this behavior is likely to extend over to family business interests. It is guaranteed to attract attention, elicit a reactiveness, and engage a volunteer (or volunteers) to rescue and protect the "troubled" individual from him- or herself. This alliance controls as it chaotically diverts the rescuer's thoughts, feelings, and behaviors onto the "dependent one," thus leaving the rescuer to abandon his own routine and his own responsibilities to himself. The rescuer, having become a reactionary, absorbs the responsibility for the dependent one's actions and well-being. This responsibility extends to experiencing feelings of anxiety, pity, and possible guilt over the dependent's problem. This alliance can be labeled dependent bonding, and may be interpreted as payment for what is perceived to be overdue with reference to this dyad relationship. This, in turn, vicariously fulfills recognition hunger.

Achieving power by creating dependency in others is characterized by regularly engaging in behavior with intent to undermine another's self-confidence and self-reliance. This relationship can also be labeled dependent bonding. The individual seeking control in this dyad relationship does so by attempting to create a feeling of self-doubt in the "dependent one" through advice-giving, coercion, guilt, or domination. The one in the control position believes that she knows what is best for the other and puts her efforts into influencing how events turn out. This individual (in the control position) lives life feeling threatened by loss, and as such, will be overly tolerant of inappropriate behavior. This is due to the fact that the one controlling is dependent upon this relationship, because she thinks that the "dependent one" will provide the happiness, love, and approval which she herself is seeking. This, in turn, also vicariously fulfills recognition hunger.

The reality of achieving control in a dependent bonding relationship is that the ones who appear to be in control are in fact controlled themselves. The social payoff for these three relationship control styles (The Restrictive, The Demanding, and The Oppressive) is that situations appear to be predictable and familiar. Others conform, and one's self-image is artificially heightened by the belief that he or she has "won," even though it is at another's expense. The similarities of these three relationship control styles is observed through the tactics which one employs to obtain control. These destructive tactics are as follows:

47

Tactic One: Acknowledge who is in control.
- Employ fault-finding; invite others to feel negative, inadequate, and dissatisfied with their own self-image; instill and reinforce a lack of self-confidence.
- Project self as having power, which serves to compensate for feelings of powerlessness in other areas of life.

Tactic Two: Reinforce dependence.
- Instill self-doubt in others.
- Project self as being right.
- Discourage self-reliance.

Tactic Three: Manipulate the feelings of others.
- Give the hidden, underlying message: "I don't want you to feel too competent or too capable, the result of which is that you'd go off on your own and achieve, leaving me/us behind."
- Employ the use of guilt.

All three relationship control styles operate under the belief that the world is not a safe place.

- The Restrictive Control Style has passed on a lesson through the manipulations of: "Doubt yourself. Rely upon me."
- The Demanding Control Style has passed on a lesson through the manipulations of: "Demonstrate your love and your loyalty. Rescue and protect me."
- The Oppressive Control Style has passed on a lesson through the manipulations of: "Don't question my authority. Just do as I say or suffer the consequences."

All three relationship control styles believe that there is room for only one leader, and the individuals who are proponents of these tactics have assigned themselves as that leader. There is likewise a double standard that operates for those who believe that they are in control or in power. They make the rules of the game, but they don't necessarily follow them. "Do as I say, not as I do," is professed. "Accept the status quo; reject the self," is also professed, but in subtle ways. Bear in mind that these relationship control styles are presented from the facade, the projected image, that the one fostering dependency in another is doing so out of love. The reality is that these people are motivated by fear.

Please remember as you continue to educate yourself on these dynamics that all is not frozen; one is not *always* in a role of restrictor, demander, or oppressor. What dominates is how rooted the seeds of thought are concerning the rules of the relationship and the negative consequences that one can anticipate for not participating. For most, the negative consequence is primarily a fear of abandonment—of being discarded, thrown away, invisible. The ultimate manipulation is the deviousness in asserting the message that "the world is not a safe place." The one being manipulated comes to believe that he or she is dependent upon the one doing the manipulating. In fact, the one doing the manipulating is doing so out of his or her own fears of managing in the world alone.

In the **Restrictive Control Style**, the lesson of:

"Doubt yourself. Rely upon me."

is actually a hidden message of:

"I can't make it alone. I need you to need me, so that I can focus on your needs instead of addressing what's really going on within me."

In the **Demanding Control Style**, the lesson of:

"Demonstrate your love and your loyalty. Rescue and protect me."

is actually a hidden message of:

"If anything happens to me, it will be your fault. You were supposed to be responsible."

In the **Oppressive Control Style**, the lesson of:

"Don't question my authority. Just do as I say or suffer the consequences."

is actually a hidden message of:

"When I am not obeyed and I can't cope with frustration, I make everyone else suffer for my powerlessness."

It is important to note that these control styles can manifest a lack of control through abuse of alcohol, abuse of drugs, gambling, or other self-destructive behaviors which are professed to be retaliatory actions against others who are blamed for provoking and causing the "restricting," "demanding," or "oppressing" individual to be out-of-control. This individual abhors his or her own weakness and, when evidenced, makes everyone else suffer.

The above control styles involve **manipulation**, meaning

that a person is controlling another through unfair means to serve his or her own advantage. When one manipulates, he or she holds another in disrespect and low esteem and profits by playing upon the other's vulnerabilities. It is the means by which one lures another into a compromising position. The fact that it is harmful (not in the best interest of the one being manipulated) is balanced by the fact that it is enticing. The activity of luring another into one's power-trap is done so by perceiving that the "lure-ee" is manipulatable. This is not a one-sided arrangement. Blame cannot be assigned to the manipulator if one is choosing to let him- or herself be manipulated, perhaps subconsciously wanting to be rescued from his or her own vulnerabilities and fears. Each participant has self-defined wants and desires.

Thus, in these relationship control styles, the power of control comes from "one up—one down;" the participants are not functioning as equals. Relationships which operate under these rigidly defined conditions lack genuine connectedness. Individuals are emotionally divided. One "belongs" by abiding by the rules—playing the agreed upon roles as defined by the system without making waves.

Security and happiness are seen as coming from external factors. When needs go unfulfilled, it is easier to blame others, indulge in self-pity, and be angry. The loyalty that is given to this dis-eased system is sabotaging the loyalty that one needs to extend to oneself. Loyalty is then displaced when one chooses to give up self-control and becomes dependent, allowing oneself to be manipulated. It is one thing for a family member to make compromises for another, to situationally forego a personally desired outcome for a happy medium. It is another thing to be compromised—to endanger, discredit, or abandon oneself. Yet, as a family member of a closed relationship configuration, one is not expected to be self-reliant, a wave-maker, or a risk-taker. One is expected to be dependent.

Forming a Coalition: A Struggle for Power

Let us now move on to what happens when it is apparent that someone is not "getting his/her way." When unrealistic expectations lead to a struggle for power, the next line of defense is to bring in a third person for leverage. Drawing in this third person when there is duress is called *forming a coalition*. A **coalition** is defined as a temporary alliance of a *distinct* individual for the purpose of giving aid in reassigning the "ratio of power" to the twosome system. The word "distinct" is particularly important because one would not seek out a third-party who would work against one's desired outcome. One selects a third-party who supplies what he or she lacks and, at the same time, shares a mutual dependence.

This joining together of the two people in relation to a third is defined as a triangular relationship. Thomas Fogerty (1996) was the first to study the dynamic of relationship movement in the pattern of triangles. Fogerty perceived that it is directly due to feeling a lack of emotional security in one's relationship with another (a second individual) that causes one to create distance—to decrease discomfort and tension. Thus, one brings in a third individual not only to refocus one's energies, but to readjust one's emotional balance when one is feeling conflicted.

As you begin to gain clarity with regard to your own family system, you will be able to identify your own relationship triangles. It is a noticeable pattern of behavior, and it becomes predictable over time. We create triangles as a form of self-preservation, an instinctive tendency to regulate and protect our existence from anticipated emotional harm. This self-preservation leads us in search of a comfortable relationship space, not only with ourselves and our roles as participants in a family-run business, but also with the relationships that we have with others. It is an attempt to tenuously balance our recognition hunger with our comfort zone. The need for self-gratification is approached through attention-getting behavior. Yet a self-regulated emotional distance is maintained to keep anticipated emotional discomfort and/or negative consequences at bay. This self-regulating, self-preserving balancing act serves to calm our internalized conflict of anxiety and fear.

Some of your triangles will seem obvious; others will be less obvious. Likewise, the reasons for the formations of such triangles may be clear or unclear. However, the behavior is purposeful: to attempt to make your environment as emotionally safe as possible. Thus, while self-preservation can be seen as having honorable intentions, triangles can also be considered a *blurring of boundaries*. Boundaries are end points, and therefore, boundaries are not without measure. You measure a relationship in a dyad by: (a) showing positive regard for the other individual; (b) exchanging information and expressing feelings; and (c) conveying and settling differences. While boundaries in a relationship are invisible, there is a line of demarcation. When you cross the line, you are sending a message to the other individual in the dyad that he or she is not important. The result is that you soil the heart of the relationship. Thus, blurring of boundaries means that you went too far. Triangulating a third person into the dyad is invasive. Genuine connectedness is not possible. When the dyad is undermined, it deteriorates, which in turn works against developing and maintaining a healthy twosome relationship. Consequently, when a third person is triangulated into the dyad, it is to *take sides* with one of the individuals in the twosome relationship. It is "taking sides" that keeps triangles in operation. In a family, it is not always easy to be emotionally neutral, to not take sides, especially when strong feelings are involved. For this reason, the formation of relationship triangles is self-defeating and self-sabotaging, rather than self-preserving. If triangles are for the purpose of readjusting one's emotional balance when one is feeling conflicted, then the higher the discomfort, the more creative one becomes in manipulating and controlling one's environment and others.

All relationship triangles are by their very nature motivated by a need to gain power and influence and a need to avoid loss. On a covert level, one is self-conscious and ill-at-ease. To compensate on an overt level, focus is on being self-serving; cooperative intentions are lacking; concern is for one's own being. The end, one believes, can sometimes justify the means. One becomes self-involved, preoccupied with oneself, concentrating on one's own advantage without regard for others. One becomes self-propelled and self-indulgent, with focus on excessive and unrestrained gratification of one's own desires. Given this perspective, triangulated relationships provoke feelings and behaviors in others that direct attention away from forming a cohesive work environment.

A family-run business is not self-sustaining. It is dependent, unable to maintain itself without the effort of its major contributing players. *One is not self-supporting in a family-run business.* Family-run business represents established interdependence. However, if one is operating from a closed relationship configuration, there is no interdependence; power and influence are self-involved and self-propelled. A price is paid for self-defense and the attempt at self-preservation. By underestimating the capacity to be interdependent, to be a team, one sells out, betraying not just oneself, but the family-run business as well. The roles played and the triangles formed influence the course of the family-run business' well-being and one's personal well-being.

Murray Bowen (1994) notes, "When tensions are very high in families and available family triangles are exhausted, the family triangles in people from outside the family" (p.374). In one's family-run business, conflicts can be acted out by entangling selected hired staff or even relevant outside business associates. It is both natural and predictable that in any emotionally involved relationship, conflicting needs do occur, regardless of how developmentally evolved the people are as communicators. Monica McGoldrick and Randy Gerson (1985), through interpreting Bowen, acknowledge, "When there is high tension in a system, it is common for two people to join in relating to a third to relieve stress. However, healthy development means differentiating to the point where one relates on an individualized basis rather than on the basis of the relationship that person has to someone else" (p.98). In other words, this "relating to a third to relieve stress" in healthy development is not used as a line of defense. For the individual who has been able to differentiate from the family, relating to a third is not: (a) a tactic for leverage to enhance one's persuasion capacity; (b) a tactic to elicit from another the pressured choice of taking sides; or (c) a tactic to manipulate and to control one's environment, as well as others. Relating to a third is merely seeking a comfortable relationship space from the emotional discomfort of the dyad (two-person) relationship. When one is differentiated and relating on an individualized basis, the intent is to "self"-realign, not to "other"-realign.

In a closed family system, communication patterns that are reflected in individual performance styles, in dyad relationship control styles, and in one's coalitions through triangulations, are employed as vehicles to cope with difficulties in a family divided. It is a personal response to attempt to control the impact of the environmental dis-ease. Genuine opportunities for growth (differentiation and interdependence) are not built into the closed family system business environment. The intent to problem-solve unfortunately results in a system filled with problem-maintaining behaviors, complicating that which was initially dissatisfying.

To continue in maladaptive games in a business setting not only freezes one's natural developmental course, but strongly represents a resistance to developing as a team. The result is that family busy-ness competes with family business.

CHAPTER SIX:

RECIPE INGREDIENT FOR A FAMILY'S EMOTIONAL SYSTEM– RULES

> - Self-Worth
> - Communication
> - **Rules**
> - Beliefs

One of the aftereffects of a family with a closed emotional system is that it creates *discouragement* in individual family members. **Discouragement** is an attitude with regard to one's own value as a person. It is in evidence when one lacks courage and confidence to risk initiating life tasks, and it represents a personal deprivation. One is not able to truly test, define, and own one's personal strengths and abilities.

A family with a closed relationship configuration sets rigid rules of conduct. These rigid rules are: (a) difficult to grasp; (b) hard to carry out and accomplish successfully; and (c) an undesirable and worrisome burden. These rules are in fact impossible goals. The word "impossible" is significant because this *plan for being* has been created with faulty perceptions of what defines a *standard of accomplishment*. The **plan for being** contains rigid rules and obligations which generate unrealistic expectations about self and others. Phrases include such words as "always," "never," "should," "ought to," "must," and "have to." **Standards of accomplishment** are assessed by concluding whether or not these rigid rules of conduct are met.

Rules are required to be obeyed in order to secure a position in the family and be seen as "acceptable" by adult parental authority figures. As a comparative, these rules are impossible to carry out and accomplish successfully, because rigid rules of conduct undermine not only one's ability to identify, clarify, and achieve goals, but they also undermine the energy and enthusiasm required to carry one's directed efforts toward one's designated intention.

Over time, these rigid rules of conduct condition one to perceive oneself, one's interactions with others, and one's walk through life with a distorted outlook; efforts are evaluated by all-or-nothing thinking. "I'm a perfectionist," gets said with pride, as it implies that one sets high standards. One comes to equate being a perfectionist or having perfectionist thinking as positive attributes. In reality, if one's standards and one's rules of conduct are to be perfect, then one is left with no room for trial-and-error; either one is perfect, or one is a failure. There are no opportunities allotted for "becoming,"—for the process of evolving. This conditioned response to evaluating performance in all-or-nothing thinking can easily lead to living an anxious, frustrated, angry, and unfulfilled life, brought about by a restless impatience when one is forced to experience opposition or delays in desired gratification.

These strict expectations, these intolerances for mistakes, these rigid rules of conduct, and these unreasonable demands for success will not only be imposed upon oneself, but on how one believes that others should think and act as well. One's reasoning becomes faulty as he or she declares, "I am the mistake if I am not perfect." Those operating with these rigid rules of conduct will never feel accomplished, but rather "unfinished." These rules create a false sense of safety and security within one's family unit. The following sentences are examples of statements made when one is employing faulty reasoning.

- "I *should* give up assessing and developing my own interests, beliefs, and ideals, my own standards, and my own goals in order to please my family."
- "I *must* have my family's approval in order to be happy."
- "If someone in my family expects me to do something, I *have* to do it, and do it right the first time."
- "I am *always* expected to be similar to other members in my family. Otherwise, I am disapproved of and seen as a discreditable member of a 'respectable' group."
- "Due to our mutual dependence, I expect a return in kind; therefore, when I consider a request reasonable or believe that someone is obligated to fulfill what I consider necessary, I *ought* to get it."

These rules of conduct create anxiety, which fosters dependent behavior and reduced self-reliance in the emotional life of the family. Individuals become troubled as something lacking ease and naturalness is forced upon them. One's manner of being becomes contrived if one consistently complies in order to insure positive recognition. This creates a false sense of safety, because one is not actually fulfilled, and the family is not operating effectively as a system.

John Bawlby, in his book *A Secure Base* (1988), defines "attachment behavior" as "any form of behavior that results in a person attaining or maintaining proximity to some other clearly identified individual who is conceived as better able to cope with the world.... The biological function attributed to it is that of protection" (pp.26-27). Since attachment behavior is organized during development (p.82), the earlier the age, the more demanding is one's need for a secure attachment, a secure base. Now, let us consider what can happen when the one who sets the rules of conduct is perceived as not better able to cope with life or lacking the ability to achieve in the world, in spite of following "the rules." The observer of this dynamic internalizes that "the rules" are *not* a guarantee of protection from negative consequences. Add to this that the observer, coming from a closed relationship configuration, cannot freely verbalize this discrepancy between what is acted upon versus what is healthy; self-expression has become blocked, and challenging an adult parental figure is a taboo. One is left conflicted by the desire to obey the rules in order to belong and the desire to do what is reasonable and healthy. The reality is that one's attachment becomes tenuous at best.

Bawlby (1988) writes that "anxious attachment" manifests when one is deprived of a sense of protection, experienced by a long and/or repeated separation from adult parental figures or by verbal threats of abandonment or rejection (p.84). Bawlby further writes, "When a relationship to a special loved person is endangered, we are not only anxious but are usually angry as well" (p.79). Recognize that these youths, both in childhood and adolescence, feel that not only they, but also their families, are emotionally deprived. Children who live by ineffective rules of conduct or suffer the consequences of family rejection carry distorted perceptions of how to maintain acceptance as they grow into adulthood. They, in turn, bring these distortions to their roles as co-operators in the family-run business.

When one processes this deprivation on a psychological level, one responds by protecting oneself with defenses which produce anxiety. The anxiety is due to loss of genuine connectedness, loss of identity, and loss of self-direction. Without recognition of why one reacts as one does, and without intervention to disrupt these negative patterns of behavior, these defenses become a self-restricted way of living, both in social contact initiated with others and in social behavior that is a response to another's approach. One learns the rules of: "Be guarded in showing your true thoughts and feelings; you can't emotionally expose yourself to significant others because they won't be there for you. They are not tolerant, not supportive, not encouraging, not trustworthy, not dependable." The paradox is that joining a family-run business is a long-term, committed relationship, a relationship that particularly depends upon participants being tolerant, supportive, encouraging, trustworthy, and dependable. In short, it is a relationship that depends upon its members being emotionally accessible and developmentally mature.

Family members tend to carry strong emotions into the business setting. Their emotional lives in business are extremely influenced by the rules of conduct carried over from their private social dealings. Private social dealings are experiences with other family members established through: (a) one's relationship with spouse; (b) one's relationship with parents; (c) one's relationship with siblings; and (d) one's relationship with offspring. These "attachment" experiences, whether secure or anxious, will influence not only the psychological and social development of the individual within the family-run business, but also the psychological and social development of the family, and thus the operations of the family-run business.

Let us now reflect back to Chapter Five, the recipe ingredient of "communication," and tie this together with attachment behavior. One develops an overall influence style through choices in one's individual performance style, in one's dyad (twosome) relationship control style, and in one's coalitions through triangulations. This chosen influence style will impact one's primary experiences with attachment, leading to the selection of one's own rules for forming, testing, and evaluating intimate relationships. In addition, these rules of attachment also become the foundation of one's working relationships in the family-run business environment, influencing one's capacity and willingness to show cooperative intentions.

As adults, the need for recognition in one's work is a measure of being accomplished as a person. Yet a family-run business carries messages from the private life of a family, including one's feelings about how one fits within the family. These internalized messages will influence how one goes about seeking recognition. In Albert Ellis' book, *A Guide to Personal Happiness* (1982), he writes that "morality consists of two rules: (a) Be kind to yourself, and (b) Don't hurt others" (p.7). If childhood development needs are not met and the concept of personal happiness is a longing and a frustrated, unfulfilled desire, one may seek recognition by standing out in ways that go against achieving self-satisfaction. Recall in Chapter Five that individuals in an open relationship configuration will have influence styles that are partner-based, displaying cooperative intentions that are business-focused. However, individuals in a closed relationship configuration will have influence styles that are power-based, displaying a performance style that is self-focused, with the goal of having an advantage over others. In addition, this power-based influence style is seeking recognition through means of standing out by either conforming to or by opposing the rules of conduct which are established in the family workplace.

When one conforms, one gives the impression of being amenable or open to influence or advice. Actions get recognition through standing out and being labeled as one who is open and holds an unresistant attitude. In actuality, the conformist has learned to repress feelings and conquer the impelling inclination to oppose. By not reacting visibly to situations that might be expected to produce opposition, the conformist is sustained by sedating his or her mind in order to conquer the discouragement within, all the while knowing that there is disloyalty to oneself. By not resisting authority in the closed relationship configuration, the conformist appears to be easily taken advantage of, controlled, or manipulated. To the oppositionist, the conformist has surrendered, given up, or been overpowered by higher ranking forces.

Opposition gets recognition—recognition in proportion to the degree of intensity of one's resistant behavior. Individual family members who oppose rules of conduct are not doing so with the intent to sabotage business operations (to "hurt others," as per Ellis). In being self-focused due to internal deprivations and subsequent discouragement, these individuals are provoking the closed relationship configuration by flaunting behavior that is motivated by feelings of: "While I may be discouraged, I am fighting against the ultimate loss—the breaking of my spirit." Defiant, spirited behavior demonstrates the desire to be flexible and to take initiative, putting self first before significant others. This risky behavior, which is inclined toward self-healing, is misguided, manifested as unpredictable, and shown in angry, defiant resistance. The underlying message could be: "Your rules of conduct have always kept me feeling off-balance, so now the unpredictability of my conduct will keep you off-balance." Opposing attention-getting behavior can be purposeful: (a) to elicit sympathy; (b) to draw focus off of the family's distress; or (c) to show that one is not reluctant to go against the rules of conduct. Unfortunately, an added factor to this opposing behavior is that it promotes further insecurity in one's already anxious attachments. Opposing behavior is now acted out in the workplace, causing the intensity of the family's emotional tension to heighten.

It is important to recognize one distinction: the opposing individual is not "the problem." The behavior of the opposer is a response to the family relationship configuration. Those who oppose still maintain proximity, as do those who conform. Oppositional behavior is a misguided attempt at differentiation, creating a way to be (not to feel) in control when one is in conflict over exploring one's role in the "adult" world of working in a family-run business. Consequently, the closed relationship configuration is a disabling condition, for when the emotional system of a family-run business deprives its members of a secure base, the members not only anxiously anticipate rejection and/or disapproval, but their internalized wounds leave them feeling emotionally and intellectually deficient.

CHAPTER SEVEN:

RECIPE INGREDIENT FOR A FAMILY'S EMOTIONAL SYSTEM– BELIEFS

- Self-Worth
- Communication
- Rules
- **Beliefs**

The politics of a family and a family-run business are rooted in its belief system—those decisions which relate to an individual's character, conduct, and motives with regard to everyday experiences. A belief system can be constructive and serve to encourage and promote rational and reasonable interpretations of events, giving one the ability to view oneself and others realistically and accurately. Or a belief system can be destructive and serve to discourage and promote irrational and unreasonable interpretations of events, causing oneself and others to be viewed unrealistically and inaccurately. When one interprets an event or situation irrationally, the result is a tendency to exaggerate, to distort the facts.

This does not imply that all situations are positive, nor does it assume that one must take a negative situation and deny true experience by convincing oneself it was positive. It is not a philosophy which promotes "the wearing of rose-colored glasses" or "the making of lemons into lemonade." It simply supports looking at facts, at truths, without exaggerations or distortions. For example:

> Your desire is that all of your adult children actively participate in the day-to-day running of the family-run business, even though the business does not necessarily need all of the children to become involved. However, one child, the child who shows the most promise for enhancing the existing business, informs you that her energies and interests lay elsewhere. An adult-like, accurate, and reasonable interpretation of the situation (your subjective belief) is one in which your child has enough confidence in the strength of the parent-child relationship to risk hurting your feelings in order to give voice to her own needs. You, as the parent, feel disappointment and loss; this is to be expected. Your response to these appropriate but disconcerting feelings is that you acknowledge your interpretation of this direct and straightforward communication, as well as your feelings of loss and disappointment, accept your child's decision, and give your support.

Or...

A less mature, inaccurate, and unreasonable interpretation of the situation (again your subjective belief) is that you are convinced that your child is doing this intentionally to hurt you and embarrass you in the eyes of all those who you have already informed of "your" plans. This is in and of itself an inaccurate interpretation, a distorted belief. You feel that this is a disaster, although your feelings are exaggerated and inappropriate to the situation. You attack your child's judgment, questioning her ability to make decisions with the intent to undermine her self-confidence and change her mind. You claim to believe that you know what is best for your child, that you know her better than she knows herself. In actuality, you are more concerned with your child fulfilling *your* needs than you are with her fulfilling her own needs for professional enrichment and personal growth.

This is the same event observed from two entirely different perspectives—two different choices in interpretation leading to two different outcomes: one with psychological and social well-being, an open relationship outcome; the other with psychological and social impairment, a closed relationship outcome.

Albert Ellis (1962) theorized that it is not the situation, but how we interpret the situation (based upon our beliefs) that influences our feelings and our behavior. His philosophy implies that: (a) irrational or distorted beliefs based upon false assumptions and unrealistic expectations can be changed; (b) we make the choice about how we interpret and act upon our world—accurately and responsibly, or inaccurately and irresponsibly; (c) the emphasis is on the present, which lays a constructive foundation for the future, and not on the past; and (d) through discipline, one can train oneself to see oneself and events more realistically, changing one's self-destructive ways.

Reflecting back to Chapter Two, we see that if something is closed, it implies that it had in some way been open, or perhaps unfinished. Ellis' philosophy also lends an interpretation to the closed relationship configuration. A family with this type of configuration, operating under exaggerated and distorted beliefs, is aware of the flip side of reasonable and rational beliefs and chooses to remain closed, not giving consideration to facts and truths. Therefore, irrational or overly emotional feelings are clearly due to the meaning one gives one's experience, and *one does have choice in the meaning that one gives to his or her world.*

When one chooses to be irrational, despite evidence to contradict and alter distortions in beliefs, one is indeed closed. While alternative ingredients are available, the family with a closed relationship configuration resists changing the traditional, unhealthy, and unfulfilling recipe to maintain the status quo. What is particularly disheartening is that the price for *not* altering the recipe to healthier ingredients results in self-punishment—the unintended negative consequences that are a natural and logical progression of irrational beliefs.

Let us now return to the example of how you as a parent interpret and respond to the disclosure by your child of her not joining the family-run business.

Having an open relationship interaction results in positive consequences. Your child feels understood, and you, as the parent, feel understood. Each of you has walked away with closure. There is no need to second-guess or to mind-read, since communication is direct. Due to the outcome of this interaction, your child can feel safe in approaching you in the future if she wants a career change, perhaps joining the family-run business at a later date.

However...

Having a closed relationship interaction results in negative consequences. Your child feels humiliated as you attacked and demeaned her. She feels betrayed by your apparent inability to be supportive. Feeling deprived of the safety to reopen conversations, any further discussions on that subject will be withheld. In fact, the outcome of that interaction will taint any desire to reconsider her position. To join the family-run business at a later date would only subject the child to being bullied and emotionally controlled, with recognition of and respect for her as an adult denied.

Surrendering to a belief system that limits one's ability to form close, intimate relationships is self-punishing. Relinquishing the claim to form fulfilling relationships, one chooses to operate from a restricted position, blocking out options. This is seen as manifesting itself in: (a) rules that limit self-expression; (b) communication that limits conflict resolution; (c) low self-esteem thinking that limits identity formation; and (d) emotions of fear and anger that limit possibilities for risk-taking. One begins to see not only oneself, but also one's family members as psychologically and socially impotent.

Out of the closed family configuration comes the unintended consequences of individuals tangled up in an internalized conflict and discouraged by their family relationships. Rules can become a tool for the purpose of hiding behind distorted reasoning of "what is right." Rigid and inflexible rules afford one the false security of not looking at truths. These types of rules serve to control, to foster dependency, and to manipulate. Belief in these rules creates a tormented and conflicted work environment.

CHAPTER EIGHT:

THE BUILDING OF BLOCKAGES

Irrational beliefs, restrictive rules, and unhealthy styles of communication serve to lower self-esteem, contributing to feelings of inferiority and undesirability. A family system built around these ingredients may then be defined as *infectious*. When a family environment is infectious, it is spreading, or capable of spreading, a dis-ease through its interactions, either by setting an example or by words. The first is a covert method of interacting, the latter overt. The infectious environment induces burden, guilt, and/or displaced loyalty.

Burden: an emotionally punishing and tiresome obligation in which the stress on both mind and body far outweighs the advantages of being a participant in the family unit

Guilt: a feeling of inadequacy as one perceives oneself as having committed an offense whereby one's conduct violated "The Family Rules"

Displaced Loyalty: susceptibility and sensitivity to falsely supporting the feelings and interests of another at the expense of being true to oneself

A common belief which causes the formation of burden, guilt, and displaced loyalty is: "We, as a family, are only okay if...." The "if" implies giving up something, depriving oneself of something, or sacrificing something. It implies sustaining the infectious family unit through placing a value on personal inferiority by situating oneself below one's growth needs and developmental desires. It is therefore not okay to "rock the boat" or "make waves" by speaking truth and challenging distortions. In this type of system, calling attention to burden, guilt, and displaced loyalty is unacceptable.

Since it is not permissible to talk truth openly, one carries around conflicted beliefs and feelings; the only outlet for expression is through an inner dialogue—one's self-talk. Fritz Perls (1970) labeled the tension and confusion created by this self-talk as a "self-torture game" (p.15). The self-torture is created by carrying around destructive parental messages in your head, rules which are restrictive, demanding, and oppressive.

Restrictive Rule: an influence that regulates and limits movement

Demanding Rule: an intensive and taxing effort, requiring more time or attention than is felt by others to be due

Oppressive Rule: a cruel and unjust exercise of power, unreasonably burdensome and severe

One becomes programmed to feel guilty if one violates "The Family Rules." This converts into feeling obliged to not take care of oneself healthily. More than that, one quickly finds that he or she is considered disloyal when trying to set appropriate limits with regard to his or her role in promoting the family's infectious dis-ease. These areas of vulnerability and internal conflict are the cues in one's life that suggest that one is living self-defeated.

The "self-torture game" is fed by internalized "shoulds": "Life *should* be other-directed versus me-directed." When one forfeits one's freedom to choose opportunities that would lead to "me-directed" accomplishments, one learns to compensate for frustration and inner-tension by adapting in less than enhancing ways.

Table 4 introduces the building of blockages which prevent the forming of a psychologically and socially fit family-run business environment. Consider this analogy: in the construction of the human body, the spinal column is designed for the freedom of flexibility and movement to support us in the natural flow of daily life. With misalignments and spinal imbalance, we are incapable of moving freely. We feel pain and fear being debilitated as the natural flow of daily life is restricted. Likewise, the family unit is the backbone (the spinal column) of each individual family member. When all is aligned, the family is operational and able to function at its peak performance; there is flexibility (versus rigidity) and movement. When misalignment occurs, family members are restricted, confined, and in pain. The dis-ease is intensified based upon the degree of restriction in movement. You will observe that, in Table 4, the foundation block is smaller, indicating weakness. This design is intentional. Little thought is usually given to establishing foundations. As the structure continues to evolve and unfold, strain and pressure is placed upon the initial block. The weightiness comes from adding the other ingredients, all of which serve to influence the degree of restriction in movement, the burden of pressure (a top-heavy structure is not easily balanced), and the oppressive consequences which engulf and destroy the family-run business environment. Blocks placed without forethought to the integrity of the structure undermine the intent of a family to stand united. The erosion of the system over time leads to the family being divided (dis-united), and thus, a fall is inevitable.

All of these rules, beliefs, and unintended negative consequences create vulnerabilities and result in low self-esteem thinking, as well as in ineffective communication patterns which manifest in one's methods of gaining power and influence. Unfortunately, gaining power and influence through these unhealthy methods makes them counterproductive to achieving one's ultimate desires, which are to differentiate and to attain genuine connectedness.

Table 4: **THE BUILDING OF BLOCKAGES**

NOTE: Read this table from the bottom up. The initial block is represented as the smallest, indicating weakness. A top-heavy structure is not an easily balanced structure. Strain and pressure undermine the system, eroding stability.

IMPACT UPON FAMILY-RUN BUSINESS ENVIRONMENT:
- Team-building is sabotaged
- Morale is low
- Motivation is obstructed
- Genuine closeness through respect, trust, and commitment is thwarted
- Power and influence is misused; leadership lacks credibility

INTERNAL CONFLICTS:	FEELINGS:		
• Fear	• Inadequate	• Humiliated	• Disloyal
• Anger	• Betrayed	• Discouraged	• Fearful
• Procrastination	• Deprived	• Guilty	• Inferior
	• Burdened	• Discounted	• Angry

LESSON OF DEPENDENCY:	UNINTENDED NEGATIVE CONSEQUENCES:	AFTEREFFECTS OF NEGATIVE CONSEQUENCES:
• "Life should be other-directed versus me-directed."	• The natural flow of life is restricted	• Low self-esteem thinking • Needs are met indirectly by manipulating others • Inflexibility in behavior • Differentiation is discouraged

GOAL OF AN INFECTIOUS FAMILY STYLE IS TO CONTROL:	MOTIVE FOR GOAL:
• Being alone • Change • Being vulnerable • Loss of parental image • Loss of emotional security	• Lacking the self-confidence to believe that one can cope with those things that happen as a natural flow of life, one takes on unhealthy patterns of behavior to disrupt the natural order.

INFECTIOUS FAMILY STYLES FOR ACTING UPON MESSAGE:

• Restrictive   • Demanding   • Oppressive

MESSAGES:
- "I'm doing this out of love."
- "I'm doing this for your own good."

CHAPTER NINE:

FAMILY BUSY-NESS VERSUS FAMILY BUSINESS

Busy-ness and business have similarities. The motive of each is to be in a constant state of motion, to be active. Family-run businesses have goals that are the driving forces behind achieving success, toward becoming a team. Family busy-ness is also goal-oriented, but goals are not clearly defined. To be "busy" (in motion), one is in a state of "doing," but not necessarily with the goal of achieving. Achieving is usually associated in some manner with self-improvement. To achieve denotes overcoming reluctance to risk new ways of being which involve discipline, movement, and a process of change. To be "busy" does not involve movement toward actualizing potential; rather, motivation is to undertake activities that will self-protect. Being in a state of busy-ness eliminates risk-worthy behaviors that lead to long term gratification and is accompanied by conflicted feelings, such as discouragement and guilt.

When one enters a family-run business with the motive of being "busy" at performing a role for the purpose of self-protection (to do instead of to be), then one is directly competing with the business ideal. The ideal family-run business achieves value through goal-setting, focused discipline, and performance that results in the good of all. Competition should be from the outside, in the marketplace, not from within. The focus from within should be on building up, not on tearing down. Tearing down from competition within (between co-workers) only results in conflict that gives rise to tension, anxiety, and anger.

The individuals who are conflicted by their relationships with family members will be individuals who, in a business setting, are focused on busy-ness. Those who engage in busy-ness are similar to outlaws, living outside of the laws of professionalism in business, "stealing" time, "robbing" opportunities from themselves for professional development, and undermining the work culture for the advancement of "self." If a town were dealing with a real outlaw, what self-protective measure would the town's people engage in? Would they turn their backs and look the other way? Would they hide the marauder and ultimately become an accessory to the crime? Or would the town's people unite to *all* live outside of the law? Who protects the town and what it stands for?

Your family-run business is its own little community. We've just discussed ingredients—the beliefs, feelings, and behaviors—that can build a family-run business or wear (and/or tear) down a family-run business. *What does your*

business stand for? How have you cheated your business?
If one who engages in the act of busy-ness is similar to an outlaw, and if busy-ness is a form of procrastination, then procrastination is a crime against self, and depending upon the situation, a crime against one's family-run business associates, one's town's people.

PART TWO:

THE FAMILY'S "LIVING OF BUSINESS"

CHAPTER TEN:

TRADITION

When one conceives of the notion of a family-run business, one conceptualizes the image of tradition. From a historical perspective, a family-run business' goals have always been to financially support a family, to instill the value of a strong work ethic, and to be self-sufficient. From the financially struggling to the financially well-endowed, an established family-run business worked for the good of the community, to be held in public esteem, establishing a self-respecting name for the family.

The word "tradition" implies an inherited, an established, and/or a customary pattern. The purpose for upholding tradition in the family-run business is so that the family can hand down its esteemed business reputation from one generation to another, maintain without essential change the initial operational/occupational purpose of the business, and preserve both attitudes and practices. This is the ideal. In addition, the power behind being a family member in a family-run business is based upon how absorbed one becomes in the business' operational system, the degree to which the business captures one's mind and one's heart, and how one chooses to embrace the privilege and the opportunity to contribute to the welfare of one's family livelihood.

Being a family member and participating in a family-run business implies uncalculated risks. There are those people who, through a distorted sense of reality, join or start up a family-run business with unrealistic expectations, self-deceived by "what being in business together is supposed to be" or "what one desires it to be," rather than the reality of "what is." There are also many whose motives for participating in a family-run business are driven by unrelenting fears, not occupational purpose. Those who are driven by occupational purpose are prepared to invest themselves, both psychologically and socially, in order to accomplish their objectives. This includes risking negative consequences. There are those, however, who experience unrelenting fear at the thought of taking risks that could lead to potential negative consequences. Such fears as fear of disapproval or rejection, fear of confrontation or being wrong, and fear of change or failure result in the avoidance of taking any constructive stance. Those who work at maintaining fear behavior, rather than working to overcome fear, are individuals who are eroding their business' existence. The day-in and day-out operations become not a family-run business life-style, but a family-run business death-style—murdering the soul of the business.

The "what is" represents the truth of family-dynamics. Because a family-run business is a direct transfer of the life of the family unit, a family-run business becomes a unique work group. As one enters the professional work setting, one brings a long relationship history. In joining the family-run business, one makes a commitment to have a deeper, more demanding future together. Family interactions in a professional setting can only be understood by one's family interactions in the private setting. A closed family system represents more than commitment. It means uninterrupted, interactional dynamics that transfer control, conflict, and chaos into the work environment, only now more intensified since the challenges facing the relationship are more intensified. The collusions of private family life will now be transferred to the family's business life. These collusions are self-soothing tactics which only serve to further impair and undermine hope for functional business relationships. To the community, and initially to any employees of non-family descent, one gives the appearance of the united family. Yet this is a false impression, because behind the confines of closed doors, even in business, there is a family divided. The more cut off from social and community ties a family is (as its primary relationships are now each other), the more limited are its resources for addressing and resolving the dis-eases that arise, fester, and contaminate the family and family-run business environment.

Family-run business members are apt to confuse the standards pertinent to business with standards that one may extend when dealing with private family matters. The haste with which one wants to superficially address the dis-eased circumstances of the moment is governed by self-interest and a self-soothing response. From a private family matter perspective, this could appear favorable and marked by good will in spite of the fact that it is only a temporary cover-up of a much more serious problem. This superficiality is not advantageous, advisable, or wise in the long run with regard to the principles of running a business. A business does require a direct measure of performance when considering long term effects and the corresponding psychological impacts to those involved.

Remember, the honor of one's family name is behind any actions of the business. The results of one's actions are observed and interpreted by any and all business associates, whether they be employees, suppliers, customers, or competitors. When pretenses are preserved, minds are powerless to the factual, to the truth; the emotions have ruled and ruled unwisely. This poses the question: who or what is being sacrificed? The business becomes marked as suffering from a degenerative dis-ease, especially when its existence (its death-style) is being stimulated by increased activity to avoid addressing what needed to be addressed responsibly in the past. In a family-run business, "business as usual" takes on a whole different meaning.

The tradition of being self-employed use to indicate the self-made man—a proud achievement. One valued the concept of "business for profit." One profited by hard work and a no-nonsense approach to achieving one's goals. There was enthusiasm to learn and enthusiasm to contribute to one's family and one's community. Those who followed this tradition also understood and accepted that being responsible could be difficult and at times uncomfortable.

The necessity of being knowledgeable in regard to the dynamics of the family for the well-being of one's family-run business is worthy of being emphasized. A family bound by restraints, conditions, and unrealistic expectations is not a family grounded in a true profit-oriented purpose, in which the basis for beliefs and actions is geared to the accomplishments of all. A family bound by restraints, conditions, and unrealistic expectations is, in fact, a family in flight. A family in flight is running away from the intended purpose of a time-honored tradition, disregarding and disrespecting the responsibility that the members have to themselves and to each other.

The true judge of your motivations is the receiver of your actions. It is imperative to know who you are as an individual, to know your true motivations for your performance, both in your work habits and in your intentions for interactions with others. As a stranger to yourself, you stay a stranger to others, feeling isolated and never experiencing a true sense of the freedom to connect.

With these thoughts in mind, let us look at the concept of **entitlement**, both from the perspective of one believing that one has *the right to benefit* from a family-run business, and from the perspective of one believing that one has *the grounds to claim someone* as though that individual is a possession.

> **The right to benefit** is a falsely held belief that, by virtue of birth, one is automatically entitled to be a member of the family-run business, without negative consequences if this privilege is abused and without the privilege to participate having been earned. Hiding inside the womb of the family-run business or behind the title of "working in my family business" is a means of getting by unnoticed in life, escaping the importance and value of self-definition and of measuring oneself against one's peers in the marketplace of life. But there is a difference between "working *in* the family-run business" and "working *for*

the family-run business." The former only means that one holds a position in the business, while the latter implies that one is actively contributing to the welfare of that business.

The grounds to claim someone is a concept of entitlement in which one believes, "Others belong to me." This is in direct opposition to one feeling a sense of belonging in the family. When one thinks of others as possessions, one may believe that this entitles him or her to regulate, manipulate, and orchestrate others' lives. This serves to create obstacles to becoming accomplished and united as a family and creates barriers to developing as a team with the goal of achieving a business plan. These obstacles and barriers are unintended negative consequences. The reality is: *Family members are not possessions*. It is absolutely necessary to distinguish this difference if one is to be deserving of being a participant in a family-run business.

Traditionally speaking, being in a family-run business signifies the intent to **co-operate**. The prefix "co" means together, jointly associated in action; and "operate" means to perform a function, to exert power or influence, to bring about (Webster's Dictionary). A traditional family-run business is a system comprised of individuals joined together to collectively exert their individual powers in order to perform a function to bring about a desired effect. In a family-run business, as in any business, productivity is not a private choice; it is a co-operative responsibility. However, in a family-run business, the stakes are higher. One must clearly, and possibly painfully, decide what is the business' cause of operation—its purpose. Is it to be a safe haven for those who seek to hide from the responsibilities of adulthood, a shelter from having to be responsible for the consequences of one's irresponsible actions? Is it a false front to hold the family emotional hostage, to keep it bound, to restrict freedom of personhood? Or, perhaps, is it a means to distort the concepts of loyalty and achievement, to control the asserting and defining of individual interests?

The tradition of a family-run business can be a vehicle for opportunity, challenge, and growth—to explore, unite, and enrich. This requires specific components. Is your family-run business made up of predominately the needy, or solely of the able? How has your family been conditioned? What do you pretend not to notice? What excuses do you make? What are you willing to sacrifice? For some families, it has already been a business lost with participants severely wounded or destroyed.

What are your personal family-run business' lessons? Remember, behavior is purposeful. Be wary of alliances and collusions, contracts born of emotion, and the desires of individuals to distract and cover up fears. As a family-run business member, a co-operator, answer these questions: (a) For what actions do I want to be paid? (b) For what do I want to be remembered? (c) For what do I want to be respected? *Be warned: Denial does not wipe facts out of existence.* Achieving traditional business goals means thriving through one's own merit, not surviving as the victim of circumstance or the object of charity.

The decision to enter a family-run business for the purpose of devaluing productiveness with busy-ness contradicts what was once a time-honored tradition. Obtaining sustenance by entering a family-run business for the reason of escaping self is obtaining sustenance by fraudulent means. Substituting family-run business in place of the family's developmental task of learning the value of and finding the balance between separation, individuation, and togethering is also obtaining sustenance by fraudulent means. As a family in business, and as an individual within a family-run business, these thought-provoking concepts are a barometer of your actual profit and loss.

There is no way for someone to measure which is worse: overpowering another or willfully giving over one's power to another. Both are destructive. Enslaved by the negativity and irrationality of one's thoughts, a time-honored tradition is surrendered. If one's preference is to sacrifice productiveness for uncooperative intentions among members, this will lead to a decrease in co-operation, which will invariably lead to an inability to sustain one's professional codes of conduct and one's desired level of productivity. Abused by neglect, inconsistent attention, laziness, and avoidance, a family denies itself the richness of what could truly be the ideal family-run business experience. This richness comes from a blending of all that is operationally healthy in a family with all that is operationally healthy in a business. Boundaries, the setting of limits of what is and is not appropriate, are a necessity and need to be a part of the inner workings of the organization. To decide to be a family-run business and then to strictly adhere to the co-operational running of the business is not only good business, it brings one respectability.

CHAPTER ELEVEN:

"LOVE FOR SALE"

Just as there is tradition in participating in a family-run business, there are also the traditional ways that a family does things. This can be characterized by the disturbing ways in which a family is divided. In regard to family-run business, these troublesome dynamics also represent "Love For Sale." **"Love For Sale"** is an unwritten contract in which love is conditional upon fulfillment of the expectations of others in the family-run business. This chapter introduces four family stories. These graphic stories are not harmonious in nature, but rather they are real stories which exemplify closed relationship configurations. They have been chosen to bring to mind your own family's business evolution. These families are vividly striking representations of families who endured unnecessary long-term suffering. They typify families who are divided because the members used methods which were "traditional" for them—ignoring, camouflaging, and resisting—thus continuing to taint their family-run business experience.

The focal point of each story is an index person who has shared his or her personal perspective. Names have been changed to protect confidentiality and preserve anonymity. The truth of these stories is that individuals learn to define themselves within the framework of the social and psychological environment in which they live. You will gain perspective on the connectedness of the players, as well as their vulnerabilities. Critical family events will be highlighted, since critical time periods tend to revolve around important transitions which tend to influence family-run business partnering. These critical family events include (but are not limited to): *relationship shifts* such as divorces, separations, children readying to leave home, and marriages; *migrations* such as moves and job changes; and *losses* such as death, ill-health, and financial burdens.

These stories also represent each of the relationship control styles introduced in Part One, Chapter Five: the Restrictive Relationship Control Style, the Demanding Relationship Control Style, and the Oppressive Relationship Control Style. The fourth story, while it is a duplicate example of the Restrictive Relationship Control Style, is specifically included so that the dynamics of a husband and wife team can be examined. The messages received from these relationship styles play a significant role, not only in the developmental task of maturity, as evidenced by one's ability and desire to differentiate (be distinguishable on one's own merits), but in the full meaning behind one's decision to enter a family-run business.

The Restrictive Relationship Control Style:
Abel Ward's Story

Abel comes from a long family history in which family balance has always been nourished by conflict, both internal and external in nature. He sees his parents as having had a dispirited relationship with one another. The vehicle by which enthusiastic interaction was rejuvenated was through their emotional investment in their children's lives. Abel's older brother, having been an independent thinker and confident in his life perspective, was invested in and committed to the risk-worthy behavior of differentiation—in spite of any negative repercussions that would have undoubtedly ensued. However, both Abel and his younger brother were burdened by low self-esteem, lack of self-confidence, and emotional dependency—factors that served to undermine their developmental process of emotional maturity. Abel assigns the evolvement of his then low self-image to the belief that he could not compete with his older brother, who consistently out-performed Abel in school. His parents' response of, "It's okay that you don't excel in school; you're an artist" was translated in Abel's 14-year-old mind as him being excused from the responsibilities that accompanied being a student. This parental message only served to heighten Abel's persistent feeling of discouragement. Abel further extended the message of, "It's okay, you're an artist" to not just seeing himself a failure as a student, but a failure as a "student of life." In his mind, higher grades equated a winner; lower grades (not necessarily failing grades) equated a loser. This distorted thinking evolved into, "Not only don't artists need to be educated, but to be an artist, by default, I must be a loser." The message to his self-image was clear: "You are limited as a person." This set the

93

tone for things to come. The message to Abel from his parents that he could only be an artist preset his goals. Abel *did* have intelligence, competence, talents, and career interests, but he chose to ignore these signals, abandoning the value of self-nurturance until later in adulthood. Abel enrolled in art school and dropped out in his junior year. He saw that he lacked the pure talent and discipline to earn a living as an artist.

The formation of the Ward family-run business occurred at a major transitional point for both of Abel's parents, himself, and his younger brother. Abel's father had left a stable position in upper management with a company that he had been with for 26 years to risk achieving his desired goal of being self-employed. Abel had just dropped out of art school, and his younger brother had just completed high school with no aspirations of his own. Abel's mother was facing "empty-nest" syndrome. The timing of the formation of this family's business appeared fortuitous. Abel's older brother chose not to participate in what was prophetically an entangled network of continuous, self-created, conflicted dynamics, called "our family's business," choosing rather to self-define and make his own way in the world.

Abel began a 12 year journey into his family's business with his "Love For Sale" contract which read: "We'll take care of your financial needs if you take care of our emotional needs." At the time, it appeared mutually profitable. Aside from feeling blessed and relieved to be rescued from the process of finding his "self" outside of his parents' home base, Abel saw joining a family-run business as offering a greater opportunity for financial success, as his father was intimately acquainted with their business' industry. Abel also saw the title of "self-employed" as holding a social status. However, the message: "We are all equal partners," was a contradictory message. While salaries were equally distributed, the relationship was still a parent-child one.

Mr. Ward had worked long hours and was not at home many evenings during his children's formative years; thus, establishing a family-run business gave him additional payoffs. Bringing his children into the business gave him a sense of having a more intensified parenting role by being able to maintain a position which kept his adult, emotionally vulnerable offspring in the roles of children. Consequently, the family-run business, while projecting a sense of security, was confining and restrictive.

While erroneously feeling intellectually impotent, Abel did recognize that he possessed a power base in his role as his mother's emotional caretaker and as the mediator in his parents' marital disputes. Mrs. Ward leaned on Abel for the emotional closeness that she lacked with Mr. Ward. Not finding what she wanted in marriage, Mrs. Ward turned to the next available resource, her son. Her emotional void was thus somewhat diverted. In this regard, Abel was a spouse substitute, an emotional companion, someone to confide in, someone to be on her side. Mrs. Ward would state to her husband in front of Abel, "No one understands me like Abel. Abel is my soul mate." This gave Abel a position of power and self-worth, a false stability which lacked any need for tapping into his genuine substance and the inner-strength necessary for the healthy and appropriate developmental task of separation and individuation. For Abel, this role of "spouse substitute" had its early beginnings when Abel's father had worked long hours, leaving his mother to raise three boys single-handedly. Taking on the role of his mother's emotional companion, Abel benefited by no longer being the recipient of her anger and frustration. To align with her, Abel learned how to avoid her anger; his self-protected, vigilant nature could be self-soothed. All roles were purposeful. This was, in fact, the underlying fabric of collusions and triangulations. These "alliances" were replacements for genuine bonding in a dis-united family.

While Abel was receiving a disproportionate share of his mother's attention, his younger brother was "the apple of his father's eye" in the business. Abel's father continued to build up his brother's ego, even though his brother's social disposition defied all professional standards, indicated by angry outbursts, conflicted priorities, undependable work performance, and an argumentative nature. Abel's brother's marital problems, as well as his seductive addictive behaviors, spilled over into the workplace and redirected everyone's focus of attention. A pattern emerged. Mr. and Mrs. Ward rescued their youngest son and then went to Abel for consolation and advisement. Abel's input was usually focused on assessing how his brother's actions impacted the workplace. Abel perceived that his parents minimized or rationalized his brother's detrimental behavior.

Abel reflects on his childhood and his acceptance of his father's long hours at work. Yet in adulthood, even as a "partner" with actual daily contact, Abel was still deprived of his father's recognition. Professional development was not encouraged. Abel recognizes that his father's view was linear—that sales and the energy that went into sales were "the business." Therefore, his role and his mother's role— being responsible for all other areas of their operation— was devalued and seen as irrelevant. This further served to reinforce the previously existing alliance between mother and son. The legal title of "business partner" was on paper only. The only true partnering was in facilitating an atmosphere of busy-ness. Abel believes that if he had not played the role of his parent's emotional caretaker, a parent-pleaser, then he would have had no legitimate role—in his family, in business, or in life. Abel claims that he may have been praised for being level-headed, dependable, or not giving his parents "problems," but underlying this was the message: "Your business capabilities don't measure up." While unfulfilled, the risk of going off on his own was negated, as he was being rewarded with financial success. This "success" represented a family that appeared united to the outside world.

As the years progressed, the power struggles escalated. Mrs. Ward had always been "in control" of family relationship dynamics, and Mr. Ward "in control" of the business. However, Mr. Ward was finding it more difficult to maintain "control" of the business with deterioration in financial security. Mrs. Ward was finding it difficult to "control" the family dynamics. The more heightened the family collusions, triangles, and deceptions became, the more heightened the busy-ness. Keeping "busy" prevented everyone from looking at the real issues, which in time revealed a multitude of hidden feelings surrounding the themes of powerlessness and futility. The more enmeshed in busy-ness, the more chaotic and toxic were the family dynamics.

On a rare occasion, there would be directives from Mrs. Ward prompting her husband to talk candidly to their youngest son. On a personal level, Mrs. Ward's motives ran deeper than just facing the distress calls of her child. Underlying her promptings to her husband was a covert desire to provoke a confrontation between Mr. Ward and his youngest son, an act which would potentially split their alliance with one another, creating in-roads for Mrs. Ward to align with her husband herself. On a "professional level," as "business partners," there could have been a staff meeting to address the three partners' concerns for the fourth partner, with an emphasis on the priorities of "taking care of business." Instead, battles provided opportunity to restabilize the roles created in their private lives. The busy-ness was to reinforce the toxicity. The designated "problem child" was in fact just another form, the polar end, of the rescuing role that Abel played. Abel's brother knew that his parents joining forces to "rescue" him was actually his role of giving his parents purpose as a couple. Therefore, this role of "problem child" carried a reciprocal rescuing power—another form of emotional caretaker. It is not so surprising or unusual that Abel's brother had the same "Love For Sale" contract.

Abel's role as emotional caretaker took an about-face when he began to understand the detrimental nature of his own actions. He came to recognize that his mother's verbalizations to her husband regarding her connection with Abel created a distance between his father and him, positioning him as his father's rival. Feeling resentful, left-out, or jealous would be reason enough for Mr. Ward to withdraw in some way from Abel. This triangle may then have been the reason (unconscious in nature) for Abel's father's lack of time professionally for him, and his father's alliance with his brother. Abel had usurped his father's place at home. His father then could not risk his only true position of power in the work-setting also being usurped. It was advantageous to keep Abel off balance, questioning his true worth.

Abel could not totally blame his parents for wanting to compensate for their unhappy marriage. By splitting their sons—aligning with one son to supposedly rescue, and aligning with the other son to emotionally lean on when they felt overwhelmed and victimized by their attempts at saving their "problem-child" from himself—Mr. and Mrs. Ward found a way to be joined. This splitting and aligning made both sons out to be the "chosen child" ("Chosen Child" coined by Dr. Patricia Love). Thus, divided, the two sons became rivals. The payoff was that Mr. and Mrs. Ward maintained power as parents and an alliance as a couple—their form of dependent bonding. This manipulation turned an otherwise normal sibling rivalry into a devious competition that inhibited the growth of healthy sibling bonds. Abel, finally grasping the enormously complicated and painfully regretful dynamics, recognized that he had volunteered to dutifully play his part. There were no victims—they had all volunteered. No one person could be held solely accountable. Everyone had made choices. They had chosen to play out these roles, and they had done so masterfully.

As Abel's brother's personal issues escalated, impacting the psychological and social well-being of the business, Abel was evolving as an adult—a slow, gradual, but steady process of maturing emotionally and developmentally. With growing strength of conviction, Abel implored his parents to stop resisting constructive problem-solving. He tried to convince them that, as business partners, decisions had to be made for the best interest of the business. Abel urged for truths to be spoken, family counseling to be sought, boundaries to be set, and if need be, his brother to leave the business. His parents saw this as an act of betrayal on Abel's part. What Abel did not predict was that his mother would turn on him. Now he was not her "chosen child" for emotional support, but the chosen recipient of her anger.

In hindsight, Abel now understands how this change in attitude was provoked by his wanting to change the rules of the "Love For Sale" contract, threatening the precariously distorted balance of the family's preferred system of operation. The family mottos of: "Peace at any price," and "We're family; we're suppose to overlook things," were being broken. (The "Peace at any price" principle, according to Murray Bowen, is a result of "low tolerance for anxiety;" 1994, p.63.) Abel was no longer abiding by his parents' rules of conduct. He was no longer soothing his parents' emotions; he was heightening them. After all, if his brother was to develop into a healthy, functioning, independent adult and Abel was to develop into a healthy, functioning, independent adult, Mr. and Mrs. Ward would be left with what they wanted most to avoid—an empty nest and an empty marriage.

Abel's brother's destructive behavior, his parents involvement to rescue, and their resulting feeling of victimization were not as painful for them as the fear of losing contact with, and control of, their children. Abel now clearly understands that his and his brother's chronological growth into adulthood were seen by his parents as the demise of their parenthood, fear of a deterioration of a family system by children growing up and going away. Justifying a continuation of their parenting roles through seemingly innocent and enticing means is what initially prompted their family's business formation. Continuing family roles would eliminate the threat of loss. There was a payoff for Abel's brother to maintain his particular role—to rescue his parents from being faced with the disturbing and unsettling task of focusing on themselves. Abel also commented that he believes that his parents intent was to keep his brother and him dependent, divided, and emotionally deprived to better serve their needs of living under the delusion of a family united. This delusion provided for continued alliances to replace the lack of healthy bonds between husband and wife. However, Abel does not believe that they did so with premeditation or with an awareness of the long-range, unintended, negative consequences. Abel's initial perception was that joining his parents in a business would give him direction, create a professional discipline, and develop a healthier self-image. He acknowledges that he, too, was deluding himself, and this consequently made him unaware of the long-range negative effects.

Twelve years after its inception, the Ward family's business folded. Abel insightfully comments that his family had come together in business disadvantaged; each was impaired prior to the business' formation. Abel recognizes that forming a family-run business was a creative way for his parents to maintain the family unit. A family-run business was a vehicle to sustain the marital union. Abel also recognizes how forming a family-run business had rescued his younger brother and him from the developmental task of choosing career goals. Twelve years of opportunity were squandered. In the end, few rewards were reaped from these 12 years. Furthermore, to intensify this turning point, all of the family members went their own ways, financially depleted due to the events that occurred. Overall, this family met with psychological and social hazards, ignored overt warning signs, and led themselves to a devastating conclusion. Never healthily united, and now further divided, Abel views his family as actors in a 12 year play. They each had their roles and cues telling them when to enter and exit. Scenes were directed from well-scripted and well-rehearsed roles of their private family life. It had discomfort, but it was predictable and familiar.

However, this has initiated Abel's rebirth. Abel's recovery process entails his learning to understand and successfully prove to himself that he is not a disabled ward, but a legitimate adult. He sees this as his passageway to being genuine to himself, with a realistic appraisal of his true strengths, both in intellect and in developing as a successful, self-made businessman. Reflecting back to his formative years, Abel now recognizes that it was the methods of his education that were inadequate, not he himself. It took the rise and the hard fall of a family-run business for Abel to realize that a family that enters a business divided will end divided.

Abel has since received the long-awaited recognition from his father, but it no longer carries a weight of importance. In Abel's journey, he has come to value himself.

The Demanding Relationship Control Style:
Gil Avery's Story

Since childhood, Gil was taught to be competent and self-contained. Instilled with a strong work ethic, Gil was raised in a home that was burdened with the underlying knowledge of his father's ill-health and a resulting strain on family finances. Gil's father was self-employed, and in spite of medical concerns, and physical limitations, he supported (without financial assistance) his wife and four children. Gil was the only male offspring.

Gil saw his father through the eyes of a hero-worshipping son. Though his father has been deceased for 17 years, Gil still identifies him as, "my father, my partner, my best friend," an all-powerful figure in life and in death. Growing up, he saw his father as a specimen of the perfect man—a man whose strength and greatness were evidenced by personal self-control, the energy to act upon his convictions, and a capability to produce results. Mr. Avery was a substantial influence as to the kind of man Gil wanted to be.

After graduation from college, Gil was in a transitional

state. Unhappy with the working environment that encompassed his field of study, he considered his options. Moving out-of-state was a choice that he discussed with his parents. Mr. and Mrs. Avery suggested to Gil that he work with his father "on a temporary basis," rather than moving away with no clear goals or direction. Gil saw the practical side of this and recognized that working with his father would alleviate some of the strain of the physical labor that his father endured.

A year later, engaged to be married and considering the future that he wanted to share with his soon-to-be mate, Gil spoke to his mother of still wanting to move away. His mother's reaction laid the foundation for the bed of emotional pain that was to follow. She told Gil, in no uncertain terms, that if he quit, leaving his father to work alone, then the physical labor would kill her husband, and his death would be Gil's fault. His mother further emphasized that if Gil were to move away and if his father decided to close the business (in recognition of his inability to manage alone), her husband would die from boredom, which would also be Gil's fault. In hindsight, Gil wonders why he discussed this solely with his mother, why he did not initiate this conversation with his father. Was it Gil's intent for his mother to react as he predicted she would? Did he want her to rescue him from making a decision that would be a no-win situation, no matter how he emotionally assessed the eventual results? Their "Love For Sale" contract read: "We struggled and sacrificed emotionally and financially to take care of you. Now it's your turn to do the same for us." By being exposed to psychological conditions of guilt and blame, Gil was coerced into sacrificing his choices in life. Mrs. Avery saw Gil as the answer to her future financial and emotional security, the "chosen one" to secure her destiny. These psychological conditions put Gil at an emotional disadvantage that would ultimately dictate his performance style.

Having been devoted, dutiful, and plagued by fear of his father's ill-health, Gil had never taken a vacation from work. After a year of marriage, Gil took one day off of work to go away for a long week-end. He received a call at his motel on his first afternoon away; his father had died. He had been found dead on the premises of the family-run business. Gil was convinced that if he had not taken the day off, he might have been there to save his father. Recalling his mother's ominous words of only a year earlier, Gil blamed himself. He felt that by thinking of his own needs (spending intimate time with his wife), he had abandoned his father. He also felt that he had deprived his mother of a spouse and himself not only of his father, but of his partner and his best friend. The "what ifs" were haunting.

Gil's father's death was the beginning of Gil's heightened emotional instability. This instability only escalated as the years progressed. The emotional self-destructiveness wreaked havoc in Gil's personal life. Grief and distorted thinking led him to resent his wife; taking time from his work to be with her had cost him his father. Obsession with work became the object of his energies. This obsession was marked by a devotedness to keep alive the memory of his father, to make amends to his mother through self-sacrifice, and to repair a damaged sense of self-worth.

In death, Gil's hero-worship of his father became magnified, and it compelled Gil to be obedient to his mother's unrealistic demands and intense emotional outbursts. Mrs. Avery's constant attention-seeking behaviors and demands for reassurance were motivated by her emotional neediness to squelch her feelings of emptiness and dependence. This was manifested in behaviors that reflected a fear of abandonment, a fear of emotional deprivation, and a fear of losing her power of control over her son. Gil was only beginning to recognize how he would be driven to honor his father's name. His memory of his father as a source of influence and inspiration acted in concert with his mother's manipulations to secure Gil's allegiance. Mrs. Avery's motto was: "Keep grief alive." This carried a subtle, underlying message of: "One of these days I, too, will be dead, and you will be sorry." Through Gil's eyes, where once a family stood united, it was now divided.

Gil's grueling schedule, his fluctuating demeanor (from stoic to verbally abusive), and his emotional detachment from his wife became a daily powerful reminder of his loss. Gil's mother became his emotional blind spot. His guilt prevented any anger from being directed at her; he was too busy being angry at himself. Emphasis shifted from saving his father's life to saving his mother from her dis-ease of being alive. Mrs. Avery resented Gil for focusing on any observable independent or self-satisfying behavior. She was preoccupied with feelings of deprivation, and she was unable to recognize how her son was emotionally drowning. Mrs. Avery's attributes were grounded in the belief that her grief was unique. Her behavior reflected her perceived right (her entitlement to exercise her power through exaggerated emotional reactions) to elicit social responses that would reinforce her loss. Gil's torture of guilt and self-loathing worked as the weapon of enforcement. His guilt played upon his distortion of loyalty. Guilt became his virtue. His mother's initial assessment of blame matched his own verdict. Gil sentenced himself to becoming a soul lost. He came to believe that he was unworthy of love and happiness in his life, since it was he who had robbed his mother of hers. Work replaced intimacy. Displaced loyalty to his mother replaced loyalty to himself.

At the time of this writing, Gil is alone after two failed marriages—markers to denote personal sacrifices due to Gil's own self-defeating beliefs and behaviors. Gil freely admits that, in spite of his two failed marriages, being a workaholic, and compromising himself by volunteering to continue to be his mother's emotional hostage, he is still running from his pain, his fear, his guilt, and his anger. Momentary insights yield no permanent change. Gil's mind and his heart, at last reports, are prisoners of the past, and the family-run business is the jail. If his breaths of life are channeled into the business, he magically breathes life into his deceased father. His motivation is powered by the desire to make the family business into a shrine to his father, a living memorial.

Gil is not aware of whether or not his mother is conscious of her emotional blackmail or the predictable negative consequences of her wanting their lives to surround the old motto, "Keep grief alive." Gil, in rare moments of insight, can voice that his mother was willing to sacrifice his happiness for her own. Being a loyal son, he had obeyed. They jointly benefited from the alliance. A business born of the dreams of a self-made man became a family-run business born of fear, dependency, and manipulation of feelings.

What was once a proud man's lifestyle is now his son's death-style, a torment born of "Love For Sale."

The Oppressive Relationship Control Style: Diane Terrapin's Story

Diane comes from a family of considerable financial wealth and community prestige. Her father single-handedly built a multi-dimensional business with the unwavering belief that his children would unquestioningly, willingly, and appreciatively participate when they came of age and acquired the necessary education.

Diane describes her father as a man who thrives on being in control. His technique is to exercise unrestrained and absolute power, both abusively and oppressively. If need be, to reduce others' self-esteem and to discourage others' acts of self-determination, he will make a point through excess and extravagance, as in rewarding with new cars all around...except for the one who stepped outside of the "Love For Sale" contract. These purchases of extravagance are not made to be generous or to reward the predictably dutiful, but to extract jealousy, guilt, remorse, and obedience from the self-thinker. This family's "Love For Sale" contract read: "I'll only be there for you if you do what I say." The family motto is to instill the value of: "Finances (money, business) first; self (the individual) second." This motto includes a tag line: "I grant the credit. I circulate the money. I manage all investments, both human and liquid resources." Any input requested or extracted from others is a contrived tool of Mr. Terrapin's to reduce incidences of controversy and to give a false appearance of operating as a team.

Mr. Terrapin is not a failure in the traditional business sense. He is skilled at amassing a fortune and astute at high finance. He achieves this through asserting his opinions and superiority over others. He, therefore, has an exaggerated opinion of his own qualities and importance. Mr. Terrapin is self-dealing; he gives directives. Others are merely his possessions and his puppets. However, in the eyes of his daughter Diane, he is a failure in interpersonal matters. He is cruel and self-centered, possessing the cold-hearted ability to destroy what gets in his way. In addition, Mr. Terrapin is an alcoholic.

Mr. Terrapin believes that his alcoholic personality will be overshadowed by the fact that money and the desire for guaranteed security seduces. Diane, however, was not distracted from the closer scrutiny of facts, regardless of the promise of the benefits that she would receive if she were to join the family-run business. No proposition could cover up the acute symptoms of the dis-eased work environment. Diane had experienced her father in action first-hand in her personal life outside of the business. She knew to internally question: "Does my father say what he means? Does he mean what he says?" She lived with the inconsistencies of her father's words and motives. Mr. Terrapin was under the faulty belief that there was no limit to what Diane would tolerate. Diane, in her youth, did hold back from expressing how she felt about what she observed and experienced, wanting only to avoid arguments and the troubling negative consequences that came with self-expression. But she knew that she could not pretend to accept a situation when, in reality, she did not accept it. She also felt that she would be dishonest in entering the family business, after her masters degree in business and finance, without talking to her father about her reservations.

Diane reports that she exhibited self-control and courage in initiating a discussion with her father in which she spoke candidly and courteously. She agreed to enter the business on a trial basis. Diane would not be a puppet; she would not be bought. Mr. Terrapin gave the appearance of listening, respecting, and accepting Diane's disclosures. He responded that he was considering a partial retirement, and he needed Diane to take over the business. He did not trust Diane's brother to carry the family-run business into the future without her guidance and input. Diane, while wanting to accept these words as flattery, understood that this was a manipulation. She was disheartened that her father's recognition of her had come at the expense of discrediting her brother. She further claims that she knew that her father could never really retire; control would always be in his hand, even if only from the sidelines.

Diane put her energies into the business for the agreed upon trial period, reserving her skepticism in order to honestly assess whether or not she belonged in her family's business. Unfortunately, Diane experienced what she actually knew to be true from the start—that the cost of entering the family business would be to ultimately give up her "self" and to surrender her educated, fine-tuned knowledge base and her creative ideas. Diane sadly acknowledged that she would never realize her own full potential if she compromised her self-definition and complied with styling herself after her father. She gave herself permission to accept the truth. To take on such a position would mean that she would never be genuinely empowered with the full range of responsibilities that accompany effective decision-making.

Diane knew that it was necessary to evaluate her worth as an individual, distinguishing herself from her roots and her family values. She knew that she could not go through life limited; it would be self-destroying. Devotion to herself came at a sacrifice. After the trial period elapsed, Diane gave her father her answer of, "No;" she would not be staying. Her father's reaction was unexpected. There were the expected sentiments of: "Why do you think I worked so hard? I did it for you and your brother. You are unappreciative of all you've been given. Where do you think you are going to be able to succeed and receive all of the advantages that you would here?" But beyond that were the threats: "Don't come running to us when you're struggling; we won't be there for you. There won't be any emotional or financial support from this end. You're on your own now." Mr. Terrapin believed that he had put Diane in a no-win situation, backing her into a corner where she would be compelled to be obediently oppressed.

Neither the use of guilt, enticement of future wealth, threats of withholding emotional support, comments that Diane's abilities surpassed her brother's, nor statements that her contributions were needed for the maintaining of the family-run business after her father's retirement swayed Diane to doubt her understanding of truth. She had made her decision on facts rather than on emotions. She faced the reality of "what is," not "what I wish it could be."

The sacrifices of assured monetary wealth, of eventually being in a position of considerable power and authority over many, and of being seen favorably in the eyes of her father were not nearly as great a sacrifice as would have been the sacrifice of Diane's self-respect. She was not going to sacrifice years of living in self-denial, waiting for what could be. She kept her focus on her gain of selfhood.

Diane symbolizes a great sense of moral character. At this writing, she resides with her supportive husband and two children, and she has started her own business. Finances may not be in the same category as a salaried employee of her family's business, but Diane honestly believes that she has a greater wealth through the knowledge that there is no longer an emotional price-tag to her life's decisions. Her responsibility is to herself and her own family. She is honorably setting an example for her children of the kind of humane beings that she wants them to be.

The Restrictive Relationship Control Style:
Dale and Della Marx's Story

Dale and Della Marx started out as a strictly husband-and-wife business. They have no children which they could bring into the business, and they saw the financial advantages of having no full-time employees on staff, only sub-contracting out when situationally needed. In work, they shared power equally; neither was seen as the primary provider or decision-maker. Their roles in the household held a more traditional gender-role identity; while Della took on half of the business work, she also took on all of the housework as well. This appeared agreeable to both.

Dale and Della were primarily a solitary couple. They maintained a coupleship based upon their friendship, love, and mutual respect for each other. All appeared simple, uncomplicated, and pleasurable for ten years. Their motto, "We are who we are," was said with pride and strength of conviction. Their relationship appeared to be held by a unique and special bond.

The contrast in their personality styles seemed to be one of the elements that made their union work. They were complementary in nature, which proved beneficial for approaching and resolving various situations that arose in their personal and professional lives. Dale is identified by Della as "the intellectual." He exhibits stronger verbal skills, and he is guided by reason and a keen comprehension of facts, rather than by his emotions. His interests are devoted to the creative exercise of speculation, to thinking abstractly using measured objective criteria. Della claims that Dale is effective. He expediently copes when confronted with new situations in which one has to problem-solve, and he is adept at finding answers in a debate or in times of challenge.

Before Della met Dale, she was more of an extrovert. She is by nature artistically creative, trendy, and very competent. Prior to her marriage to Dale, her actions had been directed toward seeking and obtaining immediate gratification, which, in her youth, manifested in engaging in what could be labeled socially inappropriate behavior. Her attitude had always been, "I'll do what I want to do. Rules stifle me." Della had always enjoyed and needed plenty of space. Her prior interpersonal relationships with men had been stormy and ungratifying. She felt fortunate when, in her early 30s, she met Dale. She was attracted to Dale's stable, dependable, committed, and loyal qualities.

Dale and Della each saw the other as nurturants. They idealized the other for their contrasting qualities. They appeared to share compatible goals. Then came complications. What started out as idyllic was now, ten years later, turning into a disaster. Della, as previously noted, needed plenty of space. Even though she had believed that she wanted a predictable routine, this lifestyle made her begin to feel as though she was living under tight control; it became too restrictive. Dale's faithfulness and respectful treatment began to feel boring. There were no crises, no chaotic stirrings. Della, missing heightened stimulation, needed to be stirred up.

As if by magic, the tides turned. Della, using her creative and trendy nature, formed a second business. Her partner for this venture was her mother. Her mother's prompting to undertake this seemingly harmless avenue of self-expression was like an external entity involuntarily imposed upon her; "It just happened." However, this seemingly involuntary entity rescued Della from her boredom, and it more than stirred things up. The adjustments to Della's life through the addition of a new business were the antidote for her discomfort. While her personal life spiraled downward as she resumed her old habits of self-destruction, she more than maintained her professional competence. Her capacity for trendiness and creativity proved instantly successful.

However, Della's partnering with her mother disrupted the autonomy that she and Dale had come to depend upon.

Her partnership with her mother began taking precedence over her partnership with her spouse. In addition, Della's history of stormy relationships with men was reactivated. Now, their marriage not only faced the conflicting goals and triangulations of Della's involvement in two separate businesses, but Della engaged in the covert behavior of having an affair. The affair went on for one and one half years before Dale accidentally found out.

Della cites such rationalizations for her affair as not being given credit for the work load that she was carrying, feeling that she was being taken advantage of by working long hours and still doing all of the housework. She resented having to prompt Dale to help her share the chores. Dale, on the other hand, was feeling abandoned, having to hire someone to take over his wife's responsibilities in their business so that Della was free to devote all of her attention to her partnership with her mother.

Competing goals, loss of trust, divided loyalties, resentments, and deception enveloped their relationship. Dale asserts that they had never discussed Della's feelings, which were predominantly that she was stifled by too much togetherness. He had naturally assumed that his continued comfort and joy was also hers. Della had never acknowledged her discontent, her wanting Dale to share in the housework, or her needing an interest of her own outside of their togetherness. Their extreme closeness was now severed. Dale, who took pride in his ability to address conflicts and solve problems without being ruled by his emotions, was now emotionally vulnerable at experiencing separation anxiety. He was angry at seeing himself dependent upon Della for his emotional well-being, a weakness that he loathed. He was angry at the deprivation that existed in his life, thinking that for two years he had sacrificed having Della as his business partner, encouraging her in her creative venture, believing that her long hours were devoted solely to this new business. He felt betrayed by Della's affair. What he had thought of as their strong friendship held a void that had prevented Della from initiating discussions as to her frustration and discontent. Dale was angry at Della for taking such extreme measures to disconnect from him in so many aspects of their marriage.

Dale and Della had deceived themselves into believing that their love was *not* for sale. They thought that it was given freely, born out of mutual admiration and the benevolent concern for the good of the other. It was tenderness felt and exchanged. They had perceived their strong devotion to be all too unique in today's world, where talk of love is marked by erratic changes, instability, and lack of steadfastness. They discovered that their "Love For Sale" contract was grounded upon the rule of: "Act like everything is fine between us even when it isn't. Be compliant. Be closed-mouthed. Keep feelings a secret."

Dale wanted reassurances, and none were forthcoming. He felt rejected, devastated by the thought of life without Della, and threatened by the possibility of starting life anew in his 50s. Dale and Della have now started to address their complicated and conflicted life, both as husband and wife and as continued business partners. They have remained together, as of this writing, trying to sort out whether or not they can recapture what once was trust, friendship, and intimacy. At the same time, they are assessing and setting professional and social boundaries, including Della's over-involvement with her mother.

Dale and Della now understand the need for differentiation and are looking for appropriate choices for their self-definition. They are creating healthier boundaries, a shared division of labor, and eliminating triangulations (such as Della's time spent with her mother or her affair). Dale and Della are trying to break the destructive pattern of the "Don't Talk Rule." They now recognize how keeping secret their true feelings is what rocked their once harmonious system. Currently, Dale and Della entertain the notions of hope and new beginnings.

CHAPTER TWELVE:

INTENTIONS GONE ASTRAY

For many families, the love of parent for child is not a love free of exploitation. It is painful to recognize and own this truth. Parents who use the "Love For Sale" contract make improper use of another person, a supposed loved one, for their own profit and advantage. Once taught the lessons of this exploitive relationship, one can transfer these dynamics to the love of husband and wife, or to the love of one's siblings, or to any other combination of unhealthy relationship control style dynamics in which one manipulates others into feeling responsible for fulfilling his or her own unmet needs.

Behavior is purposeful and, while behavior is visible, the motivations that put the behavior into action are not. Individuals expend much energy for the express purpose of regulating their relationships, which are directly linked to their attitudes about self and others. One's **intentions**—the state of mind in which an act is done with the aim of accomplishing a goal or bringing about a result—are our internal motivators. Our intentions, therefore, are our guide to a directed choice in behavior, which is invariably related to an outcome: the desired impact, the anticipated consequences of a situation.

This does not mean that exploitive "Love For Sale" relationships are marked by the deceitfulness of dishonorable, premeditated intent. These relationship control styles are not internally motivated by a desire to intentionally sabotage growth of an adult child or a business or a family's business relationships. Attitudes of low self-esteem thinking, marked by vulnerability and fear, are the state of mind which puts such behavior into action.

In far too many cases, individuals are unaware of the full impact of their intentions and the potential for long-term (and often irreversible) unintended negative consequences. Negative consequences can color relationships for a lifetime. In seeking immediate gratification, one is often short-sighted. The tendency is to minimize, excuse away, or blatantly disregard the need to consider far-reaching effects or the reality of what really motivates one to action. If any dishonorable premeditated intent has occurred, it has been the deceiving of oneself.

The four family stories in Chapter Eleven, which characterized the evolutions of families divided, are not padded for dramatic effect. Each, standing on its own, gives a pointed view of how in the name of "love" an opportunity is promoted. But these opportunities come with a price, one so beyond the normal limits of risk-taking that no one involved could possibly conceive the ultimate extent of the damage. These "Love Rules" clearly showed that love *was* for sale, and for sale with conditions, which have implications both in the family's private and professional arenas.

- In an exploitive "love" relationship, it is not requisite that the participants engage in commendable acts. When intentions go astray, admirable traits may be denounced on the premise that this type of behavior is not associated with the desired outcome.
- In an exploitive "love" relationship, it is not essential for participants to be characterized by possessing inner-strength. When intentions go astray, one's power to coerce or prey upon the fears of another is preferred.
- In an exploitive "love" relationship, it is not valuable to have a love-relationship with oneself. When intentions go astray, it may become a necessity to abandon the "self" in order to uphold the relationship.
- In an exploitive "love" relationship, it is not advantageous to have competing interests. When intentions go astray, the preferred activity is not to divide one's attentions, but to be totally absorbed in the venture at hand. Outside interests are regarded with suspicion, censored, and relegated to a secondary (and possibly an inferior) status.

When one becomes over-involved in a "love" relationship, one becomes reactive. This means that one readily reacts as the result of an emotional upset, as when feeling emotionally threatened at the loss of control. Manipulative parents are highly skilled at hiding their true motives, that of dependency on another for need fulfillment. By the manipulator presenting herself as the helper, she creates a situation whereby she makes herself needed in the adult child's life. Presented as well-meaning, it is more subtle and concealed than direct control. This type of control presents itself in the external appearance of concern. The adult child, fearing that he will be perceived as ungrateful and thereby hurting the feelings of someone who is "only trying to help," avoids challenging this relationship dynamic. However, this "only trying to help" is exercised by the parent through masterfully instilling guilt and self-doubt with intent to further confuse and maintain control. Making the adult child feel inadequate enables the manipulative parent to feel better about herself and leads the dependent one deeper into believing that he cannot live without his "voluntary" participation. The exploitation occurs by appealing to another's fears and using this approach for one's own self-soothing gain.

Money has always been the primary language of manipulative love. We dole out this love through symbolic gestures. We buy love through giving money. We buy love through monetary gifts of value. We buy love through creating or maintaining undeserved positions in a family-run business. Or we can buy love through the actual creation of a family-run business. Money is a logical tool to keep one's adult child dependent; it is used as both reward and punishment. Especially in transitional times, one wants guarantees. One wants security, a safe haven, to be rescued. For the manipulator, it presents the ideal opportunity to create a situation in which the fears of loss of contact and loss of emotional/financial support are soothed by behavior that is motivated by the intention to discourage separation. For the recipient of these manipulative actions, the manipulate-ee, the sacrifice is worth the nagging discomfort as he or she continues to merge deeper into maintaining the rules of a closed system, which continues to hinder self-development. The balance of power is evidenced by these superior and inferior positions. Hence, *we buy love.*

The four families introduced in Chapter Eleven entered into business with biases that undermine healthy relationship configurations. Rigid belief systems held firmly in place negate all flexibility to look outside of what is an ever-narrowing tunnel vision. This filtering process creates innumerable blind-spots, overshadowing what could be healthy family dynamics. Consequently:

- Everyone's right and privilege to individual existence, including the right to experience the discomforts that come with growth, is denied. One cannot distinguish oneself from others.
- The factors which are necessary for a family to comprise a co-existence built upon sound judgment are undermined. The balancing of individuality with togethering is sacrificed.
- When one is enmeshed in the persistent emotional pain and suffering of the dis-eased family unit, one is compelled to value the family's equilibrium at the expense of self.
- The ability to honestly and readily address facts is eroded. One abdicates one's capability to consciously recognize and interpret distortions in thinking.

There is no guarantee of being free from moral fault and guilt when one is united by blood. But there is a difference between feeling a sense of belonging versus feeling a sense of what belongs to us. It is necessary to distinguish this difference if one desires to become "accomplished" and "united" as a family. We lose objectivity when we believe that being united by blood entitles us to regulate, manipulate, and orchestrate the lives of others. This only serves to create obstacles to being truly united in spirit. A family bonded by a power imbalance through restraints, conditions, and unrealistic expectations is not a family grounded in trust, mutuality, and honesty of intent. It is a family in flight. By running away from genuine connectedness, you give up your opportunity of winning as a family united in a family-run business. It is worth repeating: *Family members are not possessions.*

In the course of family life, "Love Rules" had become a part of each of the lives of the four families in Chapter Eleven (the Wards, the Averys, the Terrapins, and the Marxs); it is what these families shared in common. All of the members lacked enthusiasm, confidence, appropriately placed loyalty, and the freedom to connect. The message was clear: their emphasis on the "Love For Sale" contract was hazardous to the family's health, each individual's health, and the business' health. This unwritten but implied contract was narrow in nature, regulating attitudes, feelings, and behavior. When one's intent is to restrict, demand, and oppress, one is not practicing the teachings of love expressed, but love repressed, love denied. These "Love Rules" were then transferred directly into the family-run business.

The "Love Rules" were not just viewed as emotional components of family life, but as moral components as well. One conforms or one is seen as a traitor, betraying what he or she is taught to believe are the family's standards of right and good. In reality, if one's actions are truly moral, it would follow that morale (the mental and emotional condition of one's moral conduct) is determined by fulfillment and freedom, living one's personal and professional life fully with attributes of enthusiasm and confidence. Psychological and social well-being will emanate as a direct result of the common intent of the group. To their detriment, these four families suffered from low morale; there was neither enthusiasm nor confidence, particularly when needing to face distressing and adverse conditions. This is a state of mind which pointedly indicates that their morals—their guiding fundamental principles of virtue—needed to be evaluated and amended. These families were indeed operating with an absence of vision. They abdicated their ability to vividly conceive and interpret what was in their object of sight.

One can be a visionary. One can go beyond the limits of the closed relationship configuration and build a secure future for the family-run business based upon loyalty to self and others, positive professional self-image, and a true sense of the freedom to connect—the ultimate goal of being an "accomplished" family.

CHAPTER THIRTEEN:

COMING FACE-TO-FACE WITH DILEMMAS

Becoming a player in a family-run business is a reorientation to one's family members outside of the family's private setting. It is a time to adapt, to restructure, to renegotiate the lines of demarcation of what is appropriate to home-life versus what is appropriate to work-life. It is a period of development in which one needs to learn to compartmentalize. To take advantage of the opportunities and accept the responsibilities of becoming a member of a family-run business, one needs not only the required professional skills, but psychological and social stability. Being emotionally grounded encompasses such traits as clarity of thought and flexibility in behavior, both strong determiners for the ability to confront and rebound from potential personal compromises that could ensue. One needs to ask and honestly confront oneself with these two questions:

1. Can our family-run business tolerate the burden of potential tensions and conflicts that will naturally arise when family members merge into a business setting?
2. As a unit, can we still adhere to work performance objectives while working through these difficulties?

There will be times when addressing a situation may leave one with choices that are equally unsatisfactory. A decision that would enhance the business could complicate family relations, or a decision that appears to enhance family relations will, in the long run, sabotage the business. Coming face-to-face with these kinds of dilemmas is largely unavoidable in the family-run business setting.

Dual Relationships

Throughout one's developmental years, an individual's perception of his or her family is a reflection of self. As such, one strongly wants to believe that this mirroring image transmits only thoughts and actions that are honorable and well-intentioned, showing a critically responsible awareness and humane concern for one's family members, business relations, and society in general.

If one does not first achieve differentiation, then one may be volunteering to transition an unhealthy role status into one's career development years. This carries a potential for substantial negative consequence when one enters blindly into the closed or emotionally cut off relationship configurated family business with a pre-existing reputation for patterned behavior. One is left vulnerable, and consequently susceptible, to acting upon false convictions about one's family's rules and values. Without forethought, one unknowingly enters into a **dual relationship**. This dual relationship manifests when:

- One plays two parts simultaneously, requiring the capacity to portray complex qualities in one's personality, both as a relative of the family and as an employee of the company.
- One's individual status is at any time both occupationally elevated and occupationally restricted, given the range of contrasting situations that develop within the family.
- One operates under two opposing forces: emotions, distinguished by biases and self-serving interests, and professional judgment, which is distinguished by objectivity and the business' best interest.

By the very nature of playing multiple roles, problems will be created. Dual relationships present a complex struggle to appropriately, responsibly, and objectively address each situation as it arises, without impairing business operations. When controversy arises in the business setting, one needs to stop being seen as a family member and start being seen as an employee of the company. One is held accountable to take a stance with emotional relationships set aside and to act as a mature adult deserving of one's assigned responsibilities and position. This element of accountability is better served when one is "together" within oneself prior to "togethering" within a family-run business. At times, it may seem impossible to keep this dual relationship of family versus business totally separate. A differentiated individual will not be exempt from these complex issues, but prior self-definition will make these dilemmas less burdensome, as objectivity is already a working and acquired skill. However, while they are complicated, these challenges do not need to be problematic. *Approach all business situations with the business' welfare coming first.*

Rules of conduct serve to govern the occupational process. They need to include three major measurements: work patterns, attendance, and on-the-job behavior. These measurements provide a work performance guideline for addressing observable characteristics of job decline that are measurable and specific. Job decline requires realistic and timely intervention of a professionally objective nature. This would supersede the emotional reactiveness of one family member trying to protect another. Confronting actual behavior honestly and factually will prevent the system from locking itself into destructive models of coping with uncomfortable family issues.

Instill into the business these lessons:

- **Do not** make the issue less serious (minimizing).
- **Do not** maintain that the problem lies elsewhere (blaming).
- **Do not** offer excuses (rationalizing).
- **Do not** change the focus of the issue at hand to avoid facing what is a threat to one's occupational standing (diverting).

To gain mastery over these dilemmas, one needs to perceive one's professional world in terms of "governing processes." **Governing processes** is the act of directing the making and administering of policy to serve as a precedent over the performance of functions in a family-run business. The rules of conduct represent a deciding influence over any emotional reactiveness that would impede the psychological and social growth of the business and its work force. One needs to see the business organization as reliable, observed through set professional standards which are put into motion when required. These standards keep a smooth course of operation for the good of the individual and of the whole. This is a necessity if one is to self-define as an adult, feel empowered by one's productive work years, challenge displaced rules from one's private family life, and set healthy boundaries. It is crucial that special effort be given so as not to disrupt what is to be accomplished. This process of setting and maintaining standards graciously confronts and accepts its losses as well as its gains, and it shows an ability to master problems and not be undermined by deviations in propriety. The rules of professional conduct that govern the family-run business will then serve to put in its rightful place the unrealistic expectations of those family members who want to run a business as a charitable organization, accommodating and rescuing any family members unfit for professional employment in the open marketplace of life.

Give yourself permission to: (a) honestly, straightforwardly, and factually address each instance as it arises; and (b) define, institute, and maintain appropriate boundaries applicable to the work setting. In the business, you are a co-worker, an employee of a business, first; not sibling, parent, child, spouse, etc., first. Eliminate focusing on conflicts of interest; this only heightens the emotional reactiveness that impairs judgment. It is difficult to take a position, to be assertive, and to take rightful action when issues are blurred. Don't jeopardize the business with busy-ness. The business' interest comes first, not one's own self-interest. The end result is the elimination of a blurring of boundaries for the dual relationship system.

Old Rules and Old Roles

As stated in the introduction to this chapter, becoming a player in a family-run business is a reorientation to one's family members outside of the family's private setting. This reorientation is a life transition, a joining together in what is meant to be a constructive endeavor in which your relationships with family members extend beyond the family unit.

Long-standing patterns of behavior which were customary at an earlier time might now be showing the effects of time. What may have been appropriate in an earlier period of family and/or individual development is now inappropriate in the present. This could cause dilemmas. Generational differences will be present, but interpreted with the proper perspective, they can be of value for a broader range of input. When making decisions of a problem-solving or strategic-planning nature, efforts should be focused on achieving results and shaping the company's future.

Ask yourself these questions:

- What does your professional role require of you?
- How does your professional role conflict with the role that you've played thus far in the family?
- What rules does your business operate under that prohibit goal achievement?

Let us reflect back to Chapter Eleven's profile of the Abel Ward story. Remember that in the Ward family, all were equal partners legally, but all decisions were left up to "Dad." This was not four adults conversing, reaching a unanimous decision, and acting upon the decision together. The family members entered blindly into a dual relationship, where roles and rules of home dominated and controlled any professional or emotional development. The roles of the parents and the children in relation to each other were so dominant that they buried any opportunity for a true adult work relationship. The boundaries necessary to function as mature, responsible adults in a productive work environment, an environment conducive to learning and growing, were lacking. Any shifts in patterns of behavior that would be collectively required to achieve a professional work setting were resisted. What persisted was a collective defensiveness which worked to maintain the outdated rules and roles of the past, suffocating any chance for a future. The Ward family entered into a business, and as partners in that business, they entered a developmental window of opportunity where decisions could have become a collaborative activity. Decisions were not to be a "Dad" activity, and one was not to be "Dad" dependent. The dual relationship and the remaining investment in outmoded customs of an earlier time resulted in 12 years of collective ineffectiveness.

Issues of Entitlement

Now that we have an understanding of dual relationships and how they correspond to old rules and old roles, it is a logical next step to confront the issues of entitlement. Issues of entitlement give one momentum, as one sees oneself having the right or having the grounds to seek or claim something. Entitlement issues align themselves with one's defense tactics for control, manipulation, and dependency. As such, this is an attitudinal and behavioral dynamic and a predictor of certain dilemmas that a family-run business will face.

Others may also profit from this intended self-serving orientation. As we saw with the Ward family, "Dad" was the image employed in a professional capacity, not Mr. Ward's collective adult image, but a segment of self—his parental image. He projected an undisputed "right" to the control and power, and thus, to the position of authority. While this entitlement issue was expressed as a source of conflict for Abel, his mother, and his brother (leaving these three partners feeling professionally impotent), it also rescued them from assuming the adult roles of accepting partial responsibility in life-altering decisions. It left three partners feeling the "right" to feel victimized and free to blame "Dad" when faulty choice-making was set in motion and negative consequences ensued.

How have your own entitlement issues given you momentum? How have they motivated you to proceed in a direction that was self-defeating, rather than growth producing? Consider the definitive statements in Table 5 which are meant not to be challenged, but to encourage dutiful compliance.

Table 5: ENTITLEMENT DILEMMAS— ATTITUDINAL AND BEHAVIORAL SOURCES OF CONFLICT	
__Phrases Like:__	__Equate To:__
• "But, I'm your son."	• "By birth, *I have the grounds to claim my stand.* You'd be a bad parent to deny me what I feel is *rightfully due me.* You have no choice but to be accommodating to the attention (often excessive) that I desire and demand, deserved or not."
• "I *am* the father."	• "I am the originator of this family. As such, *I have the right* to impose my rules, my values, and my attitudes upon you. You are meant to obey."
• "This is how we do things around here." • "Because I said so." • "My way or the highway."	• "Being here first, *I claimed the right* to impose my rules upon others. I am *entitled* to stay rigid, unyielding, stuck in my ways, sabotaging advancement for the collective good of all."

133

Advanced Considerations

This chapter was written with the intention of generating an organizational awareness of how your business is performing. Two conflicting facts remain: (a) family members are *not* peers who can relate democratically as individuals; generational differences, abilities, and professional standing cannot be ignored; and (b) forming a family-run business *requires* partners to be peers who must learn to relate democratically as equals; therefore, hierarchical structures may need to be ignored. These themes of dual relationships, old rules and old roles, and entitlement issues serve to broaden the scope of one's awareness to include a wider range of sources of conflict.

As you begin to assess your entire organizational structure, you will recognize the complexities of this process. It comes down to an exercise in focused choice-making and professional accountability, as family members struggle with divided concentrations. For long-term collective effectiveness and satisfying relationships, it is obvious that a superficial scanning of weak spots is not acceptable. When one participates in a disordered work environment, one learns that one cannot confidently rely upon the business for consistent dependability, evidenced in both judgement and performance—especially when the individuals who comprise the business do not abide by professional standards. Emotional blinders, resistance tactics, and diversions will not abolish, diminish, or relieve ungratifying situations. Kept alive, these dilemmas will erode whatever positive direction one is intending to work toward. One does not want to remain invested in a one-step-forward, two-steps-back approach to doing business. Instead, this is a cycle that one wants to reduce and eventually eliminate.

Plunging into the family-run business system without an accurate or measurable account of the advantages and disadvantages that lay ahead leaves one susceptible to disillusionment. Disillusionment quickly turns into a guarded distrust when one does not have the ability to decode what one is experiencing. Feeling out-of-control, combined with the tension that comes from fear of exposure, only serves to intensify pre-existing vulnerabilities. When family members lack the ability to effectively communicate with words, the dilemmas are compounded. If perspectives cannot be articulated as a measurement to objectively evaluate the situation, then maladaptive means of coping get instituted. Inappropriate choice-making further corrupts the "living-of-business."

It is essential to provide opportunities for group and self appraisal. Constructive feedback helps to clarify the ambiguous messages that have contributed to unintended negative consequences. There *is* a relationship between governing processes and the composition of the group's style of interaction. More suitable alternatives need to be explored. Increased awareness leads one to increased personal responsibility. This leads to entitlement alternatives—those rights of conduct that are in accordance with a standard of operation that everyone concerned finds agreeable, both on a personal level and on a social level.

Table 6:
PICKÀRD'S TWELVE CODES OF ENTITLEMENT

---

1. Everyone is entitled in a co-operative venture to be seen and heard.

2. Everyone is entitled to set healthy limits when situationally appropriate—to say "no," to put your foot down, and to draw the line.

3. Everyone is entitled to make a clear distinction between making compromises and compromising oneself and to act accordingly.

4. Everyone is entitled to feel valued and respected in a co-operative venture.

5. Everyone is entitled to feel that one's family-run business associates are trustworthy when one is engaged in a co-operative venture.

6. Everyone is entitled to self-evaluate—to look from the inside-out on how one's attitudes and actions are affecting others, rather than looking from the outside-in and blaming others for feeling stuck, burdened, or helpless.

7. Everyone is entitled to discover for themselves their unique professional talents, broadening the social fabric of the family-run business.

Table 6:
PICKÀRD'S TWELVE CODES OF ENTITLEMENT, cont'd.

8. Everyone is entitled to examine the old rules and old roles that have long held differentiation and interdependence at bay, making modifications or deletions when appropriate and needed.

9. Everyone is entitled to feel that they have a personal stake in a collaborative family-run business, approaching this through gaining empowerment in one's professional role(s) and responsibilities.

10. Everyone is entitled to rationally delivered responses to their inquiries and communications and to not have to be subjected to or to personally engage in over-reactions, adult temper-tantrums, emotional exaggerations, or subjective distortions.

11. Everyone is entitled to experience new ways of performing professionally—to take measurable and calculated risks in one's desire to evolve in one's responsibilities, to make mistakes in the process, and to not be humiliated for participating in the evolution of growth.

12. Everyone is entitled, when brainstorming on problem-solving or strategic-planning, to exchange various points of view, including competing perspectives, without judgments being passed.

PART THREE:

PROMOTING PSYCHOLOGICAL AND SOCIAL WELLNESS– REGULATING CONDITIONS OF CONDUCT

CHAPTER FOURTEEN:

THE ABSENCE OF ASSURANCE

Our social world saturates our psychological states and is capable of producing abundant possibilities for our development. The family-run business is an environment where controlled conditions can influence and generate a nurturing union, or it can breed a set of circumstances that are unfavorable to the growth of the human spirit. Based upon all that has been written in previous chapters, a family-run business will embody one of the following two definitions:

Definition One: A family-run business can be an appealing occupational environment where abundant and favorable circumstances reside for adult-to-adult skill building (*not* parent-to-child or husband-to-wife or sibling-to-sibling) and for the exploration of creative functioning as a cooperative and dynamic organization. As the participating family members absorb, affirm, accomplish, and embrace, so too do they capture the essence of the glorification that comes from collective winning. Collective winning encapsulates: (a) the opportunity for expression and expansion of the family-run business' identity through the revealing of abilities; (b) becoming proficient in successful controversy resolution, which encourages acceptance of other's opinions; (c) developing interpersonal trust; and (d) creating a venue for the sharing and the balancing of power.

Definition Two: A family-run business can be a chilling occupational environment where one feels unsheltered and disgraced. It can be a brittlely constructed pursuit where careless disregard and harsh behavior are doled out without calculating the substantial negative cost to the individual or to the family as a whole. This environment produces a bloodless slaughter of the human spirit.

Based upon these two definitions of family-run business, one will want to question whether joining a family-run business means having increased freedom or decreased freedom. Was the actual enticement to be a participating member delivered under the guise of increased freedom? Some people join with the cynical belief that the closeness—both emotional closeness and physical proximity—that comes with daily business operations *cannot* be experienced without emotional discomfort and lack of freedom.

What is evident is that family members deserve to discover the true powers of their family-run business. They deserve to perceive their potential for greatness through the joy of accomplishment, the strengthening of their abilities, and the expansion of their thought parameters. Unfortunately, many merely perceive their family's potential as limited by a strained and repressed environment. The words "strained and repressed" signify members existing in an environment created without regard for the particular needs of the situation or the people involved. Rules are imposed and unnatural. Members are further provoked by fears of rejection, loss, or failure at the thought of risking verbal and/or behavioral expression that would promote self-healing. Persisting in this type of environment is a painful way of learning painful lessons.

Being provocative in a system-defying way is an indication of one's poor attempts at coping with the neglect that is a backlash of the repressed environment. Those who are invisible want to be visible. The following statements display distorted ways that members of a closed family configuration try to get others in the family-run business to notice them.

- "I vie for the competitive edge at another's expense so as not to be considered invisible."
- "I am an enabler to the irresponsible, inappropriate, and disagreeable behaviors of the dependent so as not to be considered invisible."
- "I am dependent, not just on my continued involvement in repetitive activities that lead to negative consequences, but on the alliances formed with my 'enablers,' so as not to be considered invisible."

These are unspoken subjects. In addition, there is an unspoken but behavioral competition in suffering.

- "My deprivation is worse than yours."
- "My being misunderstood is more painful than yours."
- "My road to recovering myself is more complicated than yours."

Does one have to prove the extent of one's pain by exposing interpersonal weaknesses? Each is silently waiting for someone else to take the first step. Each is hoping that someone *will* take the first step toward being an on-the-job parental figure, a learned leader. Neither age nor family positioning is necessarily requisite to be a learned leader who promotes psychological and social wellness. This role can be held by anyone who possess emotional maturity, clarity, and a high level of functional strength. **Functional strength** is characterized by a durable nature. It is reflected in one who has stamina to effectively endure the demands of a system that yearns to undergo a meaningful experience, in spite of the pains that come with growing emotionally. Functional strength is not characterized by one who advocates a purely decorative atmosphere, which is adorned by succumbing to "peace at any price" due to a low tolerance for anxiety. One needs, as an on-the-job parental figure, to rely upon one's own secure self-identity. With this security, one is then able to bring the family's collective spirit through the proverbial darkness and emerge with an assurance for renewal.

CHAPTER FIFTEEN:

WHEN MATTERS OF CONCERN GO UNSAID

Entering the womb of the family-run business does not have to be a costly investment. In the closed relationship configuration, the tendency is to be unconcerned with emotional growth and healthy family dynamics. What is embedded is an emphasis on deception and deprivation of self and others. What regrettable series of connected actions influenced this condition in which meaningful issues go unspoken and unresolved? How did it develop into a more advanced stage of functional impairment, with all concerned carrying the tension that comes from knowing of the issues' existence? What maintains this? What tactical maneuvering goes on to oppose behavioral change? Why is emotional progress resisted?

When one believes that meaningful issues cannot be readily approached (using clear and effective words that are well arranged and communicated directly, so that the receiver of the message comprehends the intended meaning), then one's preference is to rely upon language that is indirect. This means that one either chooses non-verbal messages (body posture, eye contact, etc.) or language that does not have a precise interpretation. The communicator prefers an intended vagueness so that the receiver of the message is unable to grasp any clear meaning. The sender believes that there is a risk of loss if he or she were to articulate with precise words. Usually, these intentionally withheld words surround a theme of dissatisfaction revealing one's inner-most perceptions, whether it be a dissatisfaction with self, a dissatisfaction with others, or as in a family-run business, a dissatisfaction with the work/family environment in general. One weighs the risk:

- "If I were to verbally disclose, what would be the emotional cost?"
- "How would it impact my ability to continue to be part of a collaborative effort?"
- "Beyond my relationship to the work environment, how will my disclosing affect my private family environment?"

When communications are withheld, when we conceal our emotional reactions to why we feel that we must withhold, we build barriers. Barriers of emotional distance and subsequent feelings of emotional isolation create tension within the organizational climate and anxiety within one's own physical being. Disillusionment sets in, especially when you've devoted yourself to a livelihood that appears to represent failure. One becomes emotionally tired, frustrated, and angry, not necessarily just with others, but with self as well. One engages in negative self-talk, disordered thinking, misperceptions, conversations within that focus on one's expectations, fault-finding, and "if-only" reasoning. This lack of inner-peace is marked by caution, fear, and discomfort. In spite of any technical skills achieved or validation thereof, one feels that he or she has not gained mastery over his or her environment. This is evidenced by the fact that one does not see oneself as emotionally strong enough or competent enough to speak up and to maturely express what is on one's mind or to deal with the consequences.

In most people, there is a desire to repair what one has not had intact, whether it is a healthy emotional connectedness to one's family, a heightened self-reliance, a renegotiating of one's now adult relationship with one's parents, or an overall achieving of self-identity which is characteristic of a competent adult. It is this desire to repair which creates a dilemma.

Emotional inexpression has been dictated by years of conditioning. Concerned, caring, vulnerable, well-intentioned people may feel inept at emotional risk-taking. Emotional inexpression is a feeling of loss, a deprivation, a betrayal of self and of significant others. Individuals, as part of a family-run business, each have opinions on what they perceive to be the most important areas for change, as well as the most crucial incidents that have occurred. *All of these areas and incidents have gone on to remain unresolved.* These issues, which are rarely confronted, become just another accepted way to do business; to all concerned parties, however, they remain unacceptable.

The difficulty one has with direct, honest, factual emotional expression has been conditioned by negative cultural dictates that prohibit healthy communication. These dictates, when given time, will inhibit the ability to form a trusting relationship within oneself and with others. We come to confuse the definitions of a loving gesture with what it means to be lovable.

- We come to believe that taking responsibility for other people who are capable but who refuse to take responsibility for themselves is a loving gesture.
- We come to believe that if we don't take responsibility for those who refuse to take responsibility for themselves, it will be interpreted as a negative attribute of ours, resulting in our being rejected and stamped "unlovable."

- We come to believe that saying "yes" when we *need* to say "no" is a loving gesture.
- We come to believe that saying "no" when we *need* to say "no" will be interpreted as a negative attribute of ours, resulting in our being rejected and stamped "unlovable."

- We come to believe that withholding our true feelings about the inferior quality of our family's work climate is a loving gesture.
- We come to believe that expressing our true feelings about the inferior quality of our family's work climate will be interpreted as a negative attribute of ours, resulting in our being rejected and stamped "unlovable."

- We come to believe that denying the issues that continue to go on unconfronted is a loving gesture.
- We come to believe that confronting issues head-on will be interpreted as a negative attribute of ours, resulting in our being rejected and stamped "unlovable."

- We come to believe that making sacrifices while knowingly sacrificing ourselves is a loving gesture.
- We come to believe that not sacrificing ourselves will be interpreted as a negative attribute of ours, resulting in our being rejected and stamped "unlovable."

"Love Rules" equate with the principles of "don't rock the boat" and "peace at any price." We are only seen as lovable to others if we comply with these rules. We become masters of self-deception. We convince ourselves that having a relationship grounded in pleasing others (of being seen by others as lovable) is more important than having a relationship grounded in pleasing ourselves (of being loving toward ourselves). As fear of abandonment inhabits our soul—feeling a threat of loss if we are to go forth with a healthy attitude and communication style—we forfeit opportunities for growth. We come to depend upon the intolerable. It becomes a predictor of deception; all that is not well is twisted into a self-deception that all is well.

When matters of concern go unsaid, the opportunity for emotional growth and healthy family dynamics is lost. These intolerable conditions will only be altered when one is willing to risk saying what needs to be said.

CHAPTER SIXTEEN:

ON-THE-JOB PARENTING

Being a Learned Leader

In Chapter Six, the concept of families being a rule-governed system was introduced. In rule-governed family systems, there reside authority figures—parenting figures. So, too, there needs to exist on-the-job parenting—be it a moral obligation or an obligation to morale! On-the-job parenting represents being a leader as well as a learner. This role is to set standards. To assure that family members are engaged in education and skill-building, an on-the-job parental figure also needs to be engaged in learning. Showing a readiness to learn emphasizes self-respect and respect for the family work environment—respect for self development and mutual development. Being a learned leader aids in solidifying communication and cooperative intentions. Both active and constructive participation is emphasized.

Being a learned leader endorses a standard of operating which is evidenced by:
- A sense of responsibility.
- A commitment to assessing and implementing viable options.
- Attempting the difficult or the uncomfortable.
- Problem-solving strategies which seek resolution.

Being a learned leader endorses a broad perspective which is evidenced by:
- Planning for the future.
- Goal-setting.
- Risk-taking.
- An acceptance of change.

Being a learned leader endorses team support which is evidenced by:
- Moving away from individual competition.
- Exchanging ideas in order to obtain divergent viewpoints.
- Recognizing interdependence as a necessity.
- Encouraging participating members to not only listen to others, but to build upon and own their ideas.

Being a learned leader endorses psychological and social wellness which is evidenced by:
- Self-reliance.

- An acknowledgment of the worth of acquiring knowledge.
- Optimism.
- Professional creativity.

Internal Conflict is Inherent

There are conflicting issues which are inherent in on-the-job parenting. Being a learned leader naturally draws one's attention to discrepancies in one's own psychological and social arena. Psychological activity could encapsulate unresolved conflicts with family members which, when allowed to fester, weaken one's own productivity level and call into view one's own preferred performance style. Assessing the business' prevailing social conditions could bring into focus ineffective procedures which are currently being utilized, and with this, the recognition of how this impacts day-to-day operations. A learned leader is not mechanical, not a robotic instrument to be employed, not unfeeling and disengaged. Key issues, when explored, may reveal that one's perceptions of the overall business are sound, or as just noted, they may reveal that one's perceptions of the overall business are not sound and that there are areas to be addressed.

The purpose of this exploration is to be objective, to promote constructive change once an area needing attention has been defined. When the learned leader feels overwhelmed, it is important to:

1. Keep change manageable.
2. Focus on one issue at a time unless issues overlap.
3. Prioritize.
4. Identify realistic time frames specific to each goal.

153

5. Determine how each goal is to be measured.
6. Consider who is capable of directing the process.
7. Declare solemnly the affirmation that *change is a process, not an event*.

Areas of internal conflict for an on-the-job parental figure may involve:

- Balancing one's power with one's limitations.
- Monitoring the points where one's power begins and ends.
- Questioning one's own commitment to a recommended goal plan.
- Recognizing reluctance in one's own part to seek knowledge, to be flexible, and to be open to others' opinions.
- Assessing oneself to determine if one is displaying a supportive and cooperative energy, manifested in one's actions and verbal communications.
- Over-identifying with certain family members.
- Imagining what the organizational structure could look like if the root of a specific problem (i.e. avoiding to directly address the negative repercussion of enabling a chronically problematic family member) were no longer present.
- Upholding the distorted belief that, as family members, salaries and benefits should be equitable in spite of the variance in performance types and levels of responsibility held by the individual family members.
- Assessing when efforts of a family member do not meet realistic and attainable organizational goals.
- Attempting to inspire learning, growth, and change

with indifferent or resistant performance style types (Chapter Five).

- Balancing the business' growth with individual growth.

Instilling Credibility

A key to being successful at on-the-job parenting is not by dominating, but by being a dominant figure. To be a **dominating figure** connotes exerting control through the use of forceful behavior while looking down on others, perceiving oneself as superior. To be a **dominant figure** implies exerting marked influence in a social hierarchy, selectively employed as needed, by way of effectively overseeing and guiding learning and growth. Restraint is used to keep in check any urge to mandate rules of conduct that would oppress, repress, or demand. One is required to be even-tempered, as well as to possess a rational outlook, while not carrying and exercising the belief that others are inferior as human-beings. To have credibility as a dominant figure is much more than having the power of influence. *Your actions directly influence others' perceptions of you.* Therefore, it is a privilege to be entrusted with the position of being a dominant figure, and as such, one's behavior will either acquire students or repel students.

Consider the following attributes representative of a learned leader:

1. There is proficiency in technical and relationship skills.
2. Words consistently match actions.
3. Actions are respectable. This extends to treating all family members as possessing the capability to work as responsible, mature adults.

4. There is refinement, accuracy, and a degree of firmness in the way that one's power is distributed and in the ability to assert oneself without contradiction in the execution of responsibilities.

5. Responsibilities are executed with timeliness and efficiency.

6. One is knowledgeable about business in general and one's specific industry in particular.

7. Thoughts and feelings are delivered in a concise, clear, articulate, situationally appropriate, and timely way to achieve collective understanding, unity, cooperative intentions, and proficiency in delivery of performance.

8. Trust is promoted. Decisions are not based upon emotional reasoning. Emotional reasoning uproots a business' foundation.

9. One acts calm while experiencing the pressures of doing business.

10. One treats the source of the problem, not the symptoms. One does not put energy into focusing only on the surface issues.

    a) Problem-solving is recognized as a process of events, not a singular event.

    b) Problem-solving is seen as a creative endeavor which does not employ all-or-nothing thinking.

    c) Problem-solving is kept simple. One possesses the knowledge that complicating matters encourages chaos and compounds the problem.

11. One must "walk-the-walk" as well as "talk-the-talk" to preserve one's status as a credible leader.

a) Organizational needs are stated in precise terms.
b) Goals are evaluated, measured, and reported by actual accomplishments.
c) Goals are assessed by being united in a vision.

The result of instilling credibility to one's on-the-job parenting not only promotes financial security, but also enriches family relationships. This will create enthusiastic cooperation, active participation, support and respect for company goals, and a truly united family stand—a family's legacy.

CHAPTER SEVENTEEN:

BEHIND CLOSED DOORS— PERMISSION TO ADDRESS THE "SPEAKABLE"

Speaking about what is perceived as the unspeakable is part of the credibility of on-the-job parenting. Unspoken issues are controversial subjects. Avoidance is practiced for fear of facing negative reactions. Through the use of emotional reasoning, the "Don't Talk Rule" is instituted. One has to hypnotize oneself into preferring a pseudo-closeness with family members for the presumed psychological safety of keeping feared unspoken issues from arising. Yet this tactic does not eliminate the range of discomfort (from muscle tension to panic) experienced when it becomes evident that one wants and needs to risk challenging this rule. There is personal loss and accompanying sorrow when one abandons one's needs and chooses in favor of remaining silent.

The scale is usually weighty. The family's "business-of-living" is measured against the family's "living-of-business." Without being able to speak out about specific problems, the family members, in their living-of-business, voluntarily give up their opportunity at team building. It is the act of interdependently reaching a consensus as to a responsible and appropriate direction of action that nurtures the building of a team. It is inaction—a realization that there has been a collective abdication of acting professionally responsible—that leaves one disheartened. Playing it safe does not lead to resolution. This realization is disturbing, because it exemplifies how fear regulates our personal fulfillment. Hiding behind an invisible curtain, one truly wants to engage in the risk-worthy behavior of giving oneself permission to bring out into the open "the unspeakable" and make it "the speakable."

Terminating a Family Member
as an Employee of a Family-Run Business

An environment of busy-ness is a classroom where one learns about false security and experiences lessons about being falsely empowered as an adult. Compare the student who seeks the professional and personal enrichment that can come from a family in the act of business with the student who possesses a careless indifference that is encouraged by a family in the act of busy-ness. Friction is inevitable when there are opposing interests. To rectify this disturbing and unfortunate scenario, the family may, as a final resort, need to dismiss a family member from employment in the business. This is a courageous act.

Terminating a family member becomes an issue when, over a given documented time frame:

- There have been measurable sub-standard and erratic work patterns, attendance, and on-the-job behavior in relationship to defined company objectives (governing processes, Chapter Thirteen) and the family member's assigned responsibilities.
- There has been a persistent decline in psychological rootedness.
- There has been no measurable development of the professional self.
- The individual in question is not functioning as a legitimate adult. The family is fostering a dependent, an immature adult.
- There has been a restrictiveness in the company's functioning due to displaced loyalty.
- Inappropriate liberties have been taken with no negative consequences to one's adult professional standing.

When responsibilities and performance levels deteriorate to the point in which the business begins to lose its professional legitimacy, morale is lowered. Your business motto becomes: "Constructive behavior is not required. Anyone desiring learning and growth need not apply."

Rivalry—Striving to Be the Sole Possessor

Rivalry is competing against a family member at the cost of that member's professional image. It is the act of measuring your success in relation to your perceptions of the failings of another. A collaborative effort to dispel or minimize rivalry depends upon the collective success of all involved. Each must be capable and strive toward professional and personal growth potential in order to create a business which is psychologically and socially fit. The narrow focus of one against the other or every man for himself should be discouraged. A broad perspective with regard to participation, cooperation, and collaborative spirit must be embraced.

Eliminating rivalry may entail:

- Revising relationships; connecting anew.
- Translating the concept of self-esteem to identifying and nurturing one's own personal work-related strengths and behaviors.
- Encouraging and rooting for others to nurture their potential for professional and personal power.
- Promoting a win-win mentality to create an atmosphere of mutual trust.

Not Fitting In and the Loss of Self-Identity

When one is persistently haunted by self-doubt, conflicted emotions, and the hopeless feeling of being professionally impaired, then choices need to be weighed. Should one preserve one's current standing in the business and persist at finding a way to self-define, or sever family business ties? This evaluation may be clarified if one comes to the realization that one will not evolve as once envisioned if he or she is to remain within the womb of the family-run business. To continue as is, one may not achieve an individualized existence. The direction of one's future accomplishments would be based upon the group's system of operation, not one's own internal compass.

One thing to keep in mind is that there are biases in interpreting what is valued. There *is* value in the group's collective prosperity. But there is also value in an individual's integration into the larger community's labor force, designing a career path that would enable one to prosper on one's merits alone. To conform or not to conform becomes an internal debate. There may be indications that the family-run business environment does not foster learning experiences that adequately prepare one for the mainstream.

Questions to consider:

- Is choosing to stay in the family-run business a decision based upon your desire to meet others' expectations?
- Have your standards of performance been lower, rather than higher, as a member of a family-run business? How will this be evidenced in your performance objectives in relationship to your social and chronological peers if you were to go forward on your own?
- Will self-definition continually haunt and escape you unless you venture beyond the family womb?
- Do you envision for yourself an alternative career path, and is this realistic, given your current skills and knowledge base, especially if you leave the family for self-employment in a sole-proprietorship?
- Will a potential employer perceive a family-run business background, in which you have functioned with relative independence free of supervision and accompanying constraints, not as a citation of merit, but as a threat to complying and conforming?

- Will you regret, rather than celebrate, the decision to no longer remain silent if you choose to make what you thought were unspeakable feelings now "speakable?"

You may not know the answers to some of these questions until you risk venturing beyond the family-run business. The ability to speak openly of this internalized conflict is freeing. It is both refreshing and encouraging to disclose and be understood without being judged, as well as to discuss alternatives and not be coerced into committing to someone else's goals. Take an active stance in your career path rather than passively accepting the status-quo, even if it is only to affirm your decision that the family-run business is where you want to be for now. Verbally assess the governing processes and determine whether or not you can comply for the long haul without resentment or defiance. Trust in your own decision-making. Give yourself permission to let your dreams take shape, even it means going your own way creatively and professionally.

The ultimate questions to ask yourself are:

- What do I want to achieve as a legitimate adult?
- Is the family-run business environment conducive to the attainment of my goals?
- What is holding me back from initiating the active steps that would promote achievement of my desired self-definition?

The Addiction Alliance

"Preserve the family system at any cost" is the addiction alliance motto. A broad definition of "addiction" encompasses continued investment in the repetition of

164

destructive behavior through the chronic misuse of an activity, despite negative consequences. Negative consequences manifest in such areas of one's life as physical, psychological, social, financial, and legal problems.

In a family-run business setting, the majority of impairments that will overtly manifest will be behavioral. It is tempting to define these incidents as isolated and/or unrelated to the core issue. The core issue is the repetition of destructive behavior: the chronic misuse of drugs, alcohol, or gambling. While addictive behavior sedates the one engaged in such behavior, others will undoubtedly become involved to rescue the troubled individual. Permission for all to be in denial of the problem is prevalent and observable. Even as one sees the individual deteriorate, it is easier to label the deterioration as "stress," "carrying a lot on his/her plate," or "being weighed down." These excuses imply that the individual in question is being controlled by outside circumstances. When behaviors that exemplify "let's just cover it up and act as if everything is normal" are used as solutions, the pre-existing problems in the family-run business become compounded.

A troubled individual becomes the most visible, identifiable element of an unhealthy family system. His or her behavior attracts attention, and the family members get involved. One is rewarded for having a problem and/or being problematic to the family-run business. Whether it be drugs, alcohol, gambling, or even the process of rescuing, these self-destructive patterns of operating enable the overtly troubled one to *not* take responsibility for the consequences of his or her actions. It is detrimental for all participants to continue in these roles as the healthiness of the family in business is held at bay.

To maintain an equilibrium, the business has to

accommodate. Accommodating implies either being disorganized, due to the troubled individual's professionally and socially inappropriate behaviors, or reorganizing the system by having others take on the role of covering for the one who is seen as troubled. This cover-up is validated by the irrational belief that "all will turn out for the good in the end—the way we, as a family, want it to be—if we only work it right." The cover-up is reinforced by: (a) a distorted sense of power over the one who is seen as troubled by those who have taken on the role of caretaker; (b) resistance to seeing truths and facts; and (c) an avoidance of inspecting the subtleties and the covert behaviors that influence the outcomes of the situation.

The troubled individual's disordered conduct does not limit itself to gambling or ingesting chemicals. Individuals with a problematic addiction are problematic in their relationships with other people, particularly those who enable them to continue to act as they do. There is a tendency for the addict, who comes to believe that he or she is a **dependent one**, and the **enabler** to involve themselves in high-risk situations. Thus, both become detached from operating under a mature, responsible business perspective.

The Enabler:
- *Supports* the false notion that the dependent individual is weak, and therefore supports the weakness.
- *Rescues* the dependent one from being responsible and experiencing the negative consequences of his or her actions.
- *Reduces* the likelihood that the dependent one will voluntarily seek help.
- *Discourages* independent functioning in the

dependent one because enabling discourages and prevents change.

The Dependent One:
- Is *resourceful* in justifying his/her "shortcomings."
- Is *self-deceptive*. Giving the appearance of "being in the dark" gives one the ability to remain immobilized, confused, and needy—to remain out-of-control.
- Is *conscious* of having failed to meet with the realistic expectations and responsibilities of business and personal obligations.
- Is *hesitant* to truly make amends, to make good, or to fulfill adult obligations, despite knowing that it would bring peace of mind to clear the slate of guilt and to be seen as trustworthy.

This addictive alliance between the enabler and the dependent one shows a reciprocal dependency. The dependent one's actions send the message: "I am helpless." This is reinforced by the enabler's actions, which send the message: "I will be your caretaker. I will rescue you from yourself and from your responsibilities to your professional and your personal life." The dependent one responds with an action that sends back the message: "Yes, I am helpless." The cycle repeats itself unless an intervention ensues.

Neither the dependent one nor the enabler is engaged in insight-oriented thinking. Both give little or no thought to how they got to this point or to these patterns of behavior. When limited insight is experienced, it becomes nullified with denial, a safety net to cushion the anxieties that come with accepting truths and redefining self. Denials are evidenced by such statements as:

- "It's not as bad as all that."
- "This, too, shall pass."
- "After all, we're family, and family members look out for each other."

The dependent one forms a reputation as one who is overly weak, overly irresponsible, overly self-indulgent, or overly out-of-control. The enabling one forms a reputation as one who is overly competent, overly dependable, overly available, or overly controlled. In terms of operating a family-run business, these characteristics serve to reshape business goals. Coming together and/or staying together is not for professional and personal development, or self-completion, or togethering for accomplishment, but is a bond formed by emotional chains.

Vulnerability exists in any business and is heightened in one's own business. When one takes calculated risks to move forward, one is mindful of the potential negative consequences. If one is not mindful, one may provoke and incite these unintended consequences. The attitude of, "I will be rescued, enabling me to continue in this pattern of behavior," is one that is learned through prior life events. There is nothing effective about enabling unless the intention is to make and keep the dependent one dependent. Enabling rewards irresponsible behavior and encourages the dysfunction to continue.

John Bradshaw (1988) wrote the following statement about persons being incomplete as individuals: "Two half-people create an entrapment or enmeshment, rather than a relationship. In entrapment, neither has the freedom to get out. Each is entrapped by needing the others' completion.... In a healthy relationship, each person is bonded out of desire and not out of neediness" (p.65).

Maintaining a "closed-door" policy by not giving yourself

permission to address the speakable on such controversial subjects as termination of a family member as an employee of the business, rivalry, not fitting in, and the addiction alliance, reinforces a cycle that only serves to impair and dull one's senses. Open the door to constructive and prideful operating procedures. Release what is detrimental to your family's business. In the spirit of true family tradition, coming together is to practice business, not busy-ness.

CHAPTER EIGHTEEN:

THE CONTROVERSIAL ISSUE OF THE WORKAHOLIC HOME

A family-run business can be all-consuming. Caught up in a world of business, an absent parent most likely does not realize that his or her pattern of behavior is interpreted as neglect by children who are still at home. Providing food, clothing, shelter, health-care, and money for activities is not enough. The children are dependent upon the absentee parent for their psychological well-being. Therefore, it is an essential requirement that a parent provides physical and emotional presence. With the business receiving most of the parent's attention, concentration, and time, children oftentimes feel that they are in competition with the family-run business. They then interpret this emotional deprivation as the business being the parent's priority of concern. This is further reinforced since conversations at home surround the business, vacations are scheduled around the status of the business, and sports events and birthday parties are missed due to the business. The children perceive their family to be out-of-balance, and their sense of being powerless rises as they fail to positively impact their home life through actions that would make the absentee parent(s) emotionally accessible. This is the beginning of recognition hunger.

This powerlessness extends to the spouses of family-run business members. If the husbands or wives of members in the family-run business are not direct participants in the business, their interactions with their spouses may be limited, and emotional deprivations could abound. Also feeling that the family is out-of-balance, the at-home spouse may try to compensate for feeling out-of-control by controlling the children, creating dependency, and using manipulation. Carrying anger, yet remaining submissive to his or her expected role, the at-home spouse begins to feel like a martyr. In generations past, the at-home parent was stereotypically "Mom," who became married to her children as her husband was married to his work. Emotionally neglected, physically burdened, and restricted in freedom of self-expression, "Mom" looked to her children to fulfill her emotional deprivation, parentifying a child with expectations that are neither appropriate nor healthy.

The "offending" parent or spouse may state that his or her absence is due to an emotional commitment to the family; "I am doing this for you, for us." But the intention, however honorable, has gone astray. The results can be emotionally scarring. Whether absence is purely physical, or when physically at home one is emotionally absent, being unavailable or emotionally distant is interpreted as a passive form of abuse. The children who grow up deprived of their parent's attention and recognition, due to a repeated absence of the parent's time and affection, will feel emotionally damaged by what was omitted from their childhood. An act committed with the intent to provide for one's family—an act seen as responsible by the "offender"—is interpreted in the eyes and mind and heart of a needy child as the act of a parent who is irresponsible. It contributes to an adult child's search to fill recognition hunger. This can manifest as a youngster or an adult child working within the family-run business solely as a way to be acknowledged or to form a connection with the parent. Yet this motive is lost on the parent who interprets the interest as "a given;" participation in the business by the child is expected. After all, it *is* a family-run business.

For many reading this chapter, there will be identification with this controversial issue. While the damage is done, it may not be irreparable. An individual needs to be validated, regardless of chronological age. A 45-year-old daughter may still be emotionally stuck at age 12, awaiting words or actions that could represent her parents' intent to make amends for lost time. This dynamic goes beyond the boundaries of the parent-child relationship; it can extend into how one is able to healthily master one's adult relationships. Having possibly been "parentified" by one parent and neglected by the other, the individual's development into adulthood can be negatively impacted with regard to self-concept, differentiation, and the motivation and determination to succeed.

While being a member of a workaholic family unit is limiting in psychological and social development, it can propel one to identify and adapt to the needs of the adult self and to explore possibilities for growth within, as well as to define the functional changes one needs to make with significant others. Rejection by a parent is a powerfully penetrating contributor to maturation. The aftereffects of rejection get personalized and incorporated into one's present mode of being. Healing invites one to identify and address not the limitations from an absent parent, but the aftereffects. Your emotional strength will not come from energies expended with the intent to change another individual. This is energy misdirected. Faulty belief systems can begin to be corrected by: (a) identifying one's own limitations and preferences for functioning; (b) accepting what was and possibly still is; and (c) understanding the self-imposed emotional limits that have contributed to one's destructive means of fulfilling recognition hunger.

We cannot escape our past and its influence. It will be there, creating opportunities for learning when least expected. Strength will come when you give yourself permission to invest in understanding and altering yourself.

CHAPTER NINETEEN:

THE CONTROVERSIAL ISSUE OF SUCCESSION PLANNING

Succession planning is a three-fold process which involves preparing for change, implementing change, and ultimately managing change. This process should be regulated so that the actual transition occurs at the desired point and in an appropriate way. Succession planning at its best is a gradual change, a series of steps that approaches a desired end—a rational, not emotional, process that can potentially bring a family closer together. If ill-conceived, it can tear a family apart. There is an interplay between "change" and "stability" for successful succession planning to occur.

Tradition plays an important role in succession planning. One needs to be able to hand over a leadership position in a nondisruptive fashion so that the business continues to run smoothly despite internal changes. The goal is to preserve the state of leadership through the direct passage of authority. When the transfer of authority is complete, there will be a shift of responsibility.

Succession planning is an obligation, an active process that reciprocally effects the following:

- *Maintaining* the company's original identity; preserving those convictions, manifested in attitudes and practices, which nourish the growth of profits and family unity.
- *Renewing* through the completion of one's performance; taking the daily operations of one's responsibilities and handing them over to another. Fulfilling this duty necessitates selecting one who is deemed most capable to reliably and competently complete a term as a learned leader and one day repeat this succession process. A successor is able to capably manage both interruptions and challenges without the integrity of the company or of one's daily obligations faltering. Through this renewal, participating family members feel aroused, refreshed, revitalized, and strengthened.
- *Transforming*, going beyond, or surpassing, what have previously been identified as obstacles. A visionary not only sees possibilities, but develops these possibilities to bring them into existence.

Preparing for Change

The process of preparing for change encapsulates the following three sub-divisions: stability, internal conflicts, and external conflicts.

176

1. *Stability*

Stability is most visible in the governing process. For the individual who is the representative for change (the one who is passing on a leadership position to another), this stability is demonstrated two-fold: (a) in how one directs one's influence throughout the change process; and (b) in how one proceeds to the final goal of stepping down to activate the role of successor. In choosing a successor, one wants an individual who possesses the ability to manage self, as well as to lead others. Stability implies having the strength and the discipline to endure the rigorous demands of one's appointed position, as well as the skills required to responsibly respond and appropriately take action.

2. *Internal Conflicts*

While change is imminent, it is not always easy for the current learned leader to accept this upcoming change in status and to retire or withdraw from a position that has been a vital part of his or her identity for a significant part of his or her adult life. This is particularly difficult if the current leader is the initial founder of the business. However, that was a different mission—not being an agent for determining a successor, but being an agent for building a foundation for one's family and one's professional adult identity.

In the enthusiastic quest for building a family-run business, one may not give focus to the recognition that one's position is time-limited. All at once, the years confront one with the need to prepare for one's successor. One could easily be tempted to postpone this preparation stage, since implementation of one's successor is a major life passage, a passage that could be seen solely as a loss and not as an opportunity. The reality of this transition can be seen as another reward for one's years of labor. It is a time when one has to co-exist with the notion of giving up authority, yet at the same time being responsible in exercising authority. If, up until now, one has equated "exercising authority" with being able to hold absolute and complete control, then this process of preparing for change may be particularly uncomfortable, since giving away power to another is unfamiliar. One begins to recognize the true limit to one's authority—that the business, which has always been so dependent upon this learned leader's involvement, will continue to evolve without his or her daily guidance. Therefore, one of the most enriching contributions that the present leader can make is his or her approach to choosing a successor. This is not the issuing of an order. It is not a time to manipulate, to coerce, or to induce guilt. One's style needs to be centered on being an observer, a data collector, a discerner, an alternative sorter, and a decision-maker. This is not a time to dilute one's objective with rigidity, assumptions, and emotions. The implementation of change through the passing on of one's authority to a successor needs to be made from a position of maturity and knowledge. The current leader needs to strive toward an atmosphere of togethering and to bring an added depth to one's existing position. If applicable, this process of change will perhaps evoke memories of the leader's own induction as successor to a former leader. These memories can be used to promote direction, pointing one toward a particular course of data-collecting through observation and conversation.

3. *External Conflicts*

The responsibility of being a representative for change can also provoke conflict that is external, as more than one family member may desire this particular position of power. One need not pretend to have all of the answers to resolving the interpersonal conflicts that may arise between family members. It is important to be clear in one's quest and in the range of one's involvement if choosing to intercede in rivalries. The stage of preparing for change needs to be viewed as another mark of accomplishment, another goal that requires skill and discipline. It is not to be undermined by obstacles that only serve to cloud one's focus of attention and postpone the inevitable. For those who are being considered or for those who hope to be considered, the stage of preparing for change can be interpreted as a time for competition. The interdependent and co-operative atmosphere that might have previously existed may now erupt into a subtle (or not so subtle) contest between rivals whose goal is to secure the successor position. All concerned parties (the one in the position of power and all candidates) need to remember that this is a process, not an event; behavior is assessed and qualities are weighed over years of the day-in and day-out routine of commitment to business.

One reason for this overt or covert competitive atmosphere is that, while the present leader is gathering information to assist in making an appropriate decision, the potential successors are doing their own self-assessments. They compare themselves with their "opponents," going so far as to reflect upon perceived childhood inadequacies and childhood memories of statements like, "Why can't you be more like... (i.e., your sister, your cousin, etc.)."

The official transition to occupying the successor position, the implementation of change, could elicit a grief reaction in the one(s) not chosen. One could interpret not being chosen as a sign of failure or rejection—the ultimate discouraging incident of one's recognition hunger going unfulfilled. It is therefore advisable that, as part of the stage of preparing for change, the one in the position of power not only puts energy into choosing one's successor, but remains aware of any negative reactions that could potentially arise from this decision.

Implementing Change

The one who currently holds the leadership position is also an instrument for facilitating the delicate and precise work of transitioning the successor, as well as the entire work team, to the routine of a new learned leader. Again, this is not an event—it is a process. Depending upon the magnitude of one's company and the responsibilities associated with one's position, this transition could be initiated and completed over several years time—a gradual and carefully orchestrated transferring of duties, overseeing of performance, and letting go of one's full workload.

This can also be a time for the current leader to reassess. Previously identified areas in one's chosen successor which were underdeveloped may not be evolving in a suitable fashion in accordance with the demands of the position. A reasonable time frame and a specific plan of action to acquire the necessary skill base may not have been achieved. It therefore becomes evident that reconsideration be given to one's successor. It is also a time for the successor to reassess; what was an appealing position (in theory) has demands that one now recognizes are above and beyond what one wants to commit to. In short, a "mismatch" is now evident.

Then, too, the successor, even if well suited for this new position, may be conflicted in feelings during the adjustment period. One wants to celebrate, but may in fact feel guilty for being "the chosen one." There may be an overwhelming feeling of being scrutinized by one's co-workers. The orientation period can be a time of growth and an establishing of one's comfort level, or it can be a time of burden and self-doubt, a feeling that others can read one's discomfort and secretly hope that he or she fails. It can be a time of being overwhelmed by feelings of isolation, imbalance, being misunderstood, and being lost; a time of believing that all of these vulnerabilities need to be held within, acknowledged only to oneself, and then only with a minimum of regard; a time to "fake it till you make it."

For these reasons, the stage of implementing change needs to be a bridge to support the level of functioning which the business needs to maintain during this transition process. This process is a gateway to long-term success. It is a process that will bring to light an awareness of how comfortable the chosen candidate is in operating in the new position and how comfortable the family team players are with their new coach. Examination of these issues and other sensitive areas can lead to abundantly productive discussions. This is a time to clear up misunderstandings, reemphasize required attributes, identify areas of concentration, rename goals, detail a step-by-step course of action, and make a projection as to when this change-over in leadership will be completed.

At the core of effectively implementing change is the element of awareness. Be alert in observing and drawing conclusions based upon what one is experiencing; then, check one's assumptions. After all, we cannot read minds, contrary to what many family members are erroneously led to believe! As a safeguard, when checking assumptions about a specific situation or chain of events, be sure to go directly to the original source—the individuals directly involved. Do not seek an interpretation second-hand. This could end up in a flawed translation of the events. Factually relate the situational cues that have alerted you to show concern, and express that you are seeking a response that will clarify and/or challenge your personal reaction. The conditions by which one is surrounded (and which are strongly determined by the individual in charge) will influence the life of the individual(s) in question, the family, and the business.

Managing Change

Having now gained an understanding of one's new position with all its assorted aspects, the new reigning successor takes charge. This successor establishes goals which are purposeful in nature and essential to the business' future development. The successor forecasts trends (specific to the market) and identifies the parallel series of functions needed to maintain a competitive edge. The successor also seeks and receives feedback to reinforce operating as a team and to gather viewpoints from the eyes of others.

Modifications may challenge old rules and old ways of being. It will be apparent that the presence or absence of trust will either promote or hinder a constructive and unified quality to the company's evolvement. This formation of trust, if not already established at the time of the new successor assuming full responsibility, is a nurturing process. One must be mindful to promote harmony. Encourage a contributive atmosphere, in which all participating family members believe that their welfare is regarded when action is taken and that their work skills are considered a contributing variable in the business' success. In a family-run business, it is not enough to get total support for the "top," but total support throughout. This is particularly true if one experiments with different ways of being. One must appreciate the importance of learning when assessing the results of one's efforts.

Encourage expression. Recruit new ideas. Rotate leadership when particular skills and knowledge are required for researching, planning, and implementing specific projects. This rotation of project leadership, specific to fulfilling identifiable needs of one's company, emphasizes the importance of not overstepping the bounds of one's ability. Even authority figures have their limits in areas of skill and knowledge. This is visible in one's performance.

To distinguish oneself as a genuine leader and achieve cooperation and compliance, one needs to professionally guide the business. One *needs* to take the first steps in building a term of office on a solid foundation that has provisions for "as needed" maintenance. One *needs* to build an atmosphere which is established and designed to be advantageous to the well-being of all. One *needs* to create a spirited adventure in which family members are all stars in the family production—not merely stage hands—reinforced by an attitude that emphasizes the value of *everyone's* position. As such, a genuine leader is similar to a choreographer managing and directing the various movements that create and form the family's professional dance—the systematic and rhythmic pattern of each cast member stepping-in and stepping-back when situationally appropriate. Therefore, one of the major responsibilities of the choreographer is to choose compositions which are able to conform to the particular dancers' skills and abilities. And provided that the dancers are skilled and able, they, too, conform as per the demands of the composition. To be a part of a well-choreographed family-run business is to achieve unity—it is a family whose members deserve to "dance with joy," as the act of dance is both attitudinal and behavioral. When the grouping of the different parts achieves a unified whole, it produces a work of art. Once these variables are in operation, the successor will reap the rewards of his or her labor and secure the psychological and social well-being of the company.

CHAPTER TWENTY:

THE CONTROVERSIAL ISSUE OF BREAKING UP OR BREAKING THROUGH

A Blessing in Disguise

When one envisions a family divided, one imagines not only the aura of negativity, but also an invisible label marked "failure." So, too, when one envisions breaking up, one imagines a bringing to the end that which is already divided. However, when one envisions breaking through, one perceives the penetration of an obstruction, clearing away a condition that has restrained; this is positive. When a family-run business has been existing under an aura of negativity by acting divided and being restrained by obstructions, then breaking up may become interchangeable with breaking through. It would be erroneous to label this act as a failure. In this context, breaking up can be seen as constructive, because the family has finally come to understand the price that it has placed on love. In a family-run business, love can cost.

Consider a family-run business to be a living, breathing entity. In deteriorated health, its life's breath becomes labored, its heart becomes weakened, its mind becomes clouded, and its energy is depleted. This is not referring to a business' financial health. A decision to break up a family-run business due to economic failure, in most cases, takes choice-making out of the hands of the owners; decision is then placed in the hands of one's financial institution, one's accountant, or one's creditors. As emphasized throughout this text, a family-run business is a social culture, and as such, it is imperative that a family be able to work together effectively—to create a mind-set that promotes, not destroys, that encourages, not discourages, that unites, not divides. When it is apparent that it is no longer feasible to work through the ever-increasing obstacles that stand in the way of being a family united, it is time to turn adversity into favorable conditions, to no longer degenerate, but to regenerate. Where breaking up may have been previously perceived as a failure, it can now be seen as a blessing in disguise.

Corrective Choice-Making

There are those of you who, in being divided as a family, acknowledge the degree of degeneration and the depth of wounds that have gone unhealed, but cannot consider the possibility of breaking up to break through as a means of corrective action. This is compounded by your emotional reasoning, which has led you to believe that you are in a situation in which release from entanglement appears to require more productive problem-solving than you are able to readily satisfy. This distortion in thinking has only added to the sorrow that you endure. Then, too, there are those of you who recognize that it has become imperative that you modify your view of being "the disadvantaged."

Openly acknowledging that you can no longer continue in a state of feeling weakened by unfavorable conditions is in fact a turning point. It is the ideal time for the mutual redefining of your sense of purpose for initially coming together. Initiating this activity not only shows leadership and a sincere readiness to take corrective action, but this activity promotes constructive risk-taking. You would be an advocate for setting into motion further corrective action that is both empowering and meritorious. If breaking up to break through is the direction that you end up leaning, then all can attest that this was not an impulsive decision. Rather, it is a decision based upon a realistic appraisal of the family's emotional status and on history that has accumulated over time. It is a collective perspective, not an appraisal made by the few, but an assessment by all.

Past experiences cannot be erased, though it is possible to learn from the pain of adversity. Adversity teaches one how to conduct oneself in the here-and-now, with the choice to be constructive or destructive. Assess where you are now as a family and as an individual. Ask yourself, what direction do you want to move toward? If breaking up is the preferred direction, how can you make it feasible to go your own way? Then, too, estimate the impact of staying together fractured, tormented, and deprived as opposed to going your own way. What is the greater risk in terms of loss?

This is not a time to blame. This is a stage that requires absence of blame. Blame continues to emotionally cripple, to keep one's focus misdirected, to hinder healing within, and to keep one stuck in self-pity. Seeking resolution in the present requires clarity of thought in the here-and-now, which redirects one to not be focused on the events of the past.

Appearances versus Reality

All too frequently, the face a family portrays to the community at large (other family members, friends, and business associates) obscures what the reality is: the true internal workings of a family divided. "Public" faces are put on as defense mechanisms. Fear is an extraordinary weapon to defend against appearing out-of-control as a family and powerless as an individual. In so doing, you allow yourself to become externally controlled, placing more value on saving face than on saving the core of one's being. At one time, outside intervention may have been an interceding device to propel one toward facing the heart of the matter. False pride, displaced loyalty, and the self-deceptions of, "It's not that bad," or "Time will heal our wounds," only allowed the dis-ease to fester and grow out-of-control. Now, intervention may only serve to help mediate the process of breaking up to break through.

A Trial Period

If surrendering to breaking up is not the break-through one truly desires, then consider a trial period based upon a "relationship audit." An **audit** is an evaluation of the debits and credits of the emotional life of one's business, a brutally honest assessment that shows: (a) the psychological contracts between family members, the *sources* of this estranged arrangement; (b) the social contracts between family members as seen through patterns of behavior, the *causes* or symptoms of this estranged arrangement; (c) the adverse outcomes, the *effects* of this estranged arrangement; and (d) the Lost Opportunities Verified and Exposed; the *L.O.V.E.* of this estranged arrangement.

As cause is the circumstance (the behavioral responses to attitudes such as expectations and rules of conduct) that brings about a result, and as effect is the result—the outcome, then in this case, actions and the consequences of one's actions are in question. As a family member, did you get the desired effect from the intentions of your actions? Has your emotional yield been as prosperous as your financial yield?

In your family-run business audit, you will be confronting fear, as well as critically appraising facts. Fear may have infiltrated the resilience of the family-run business' emotional system, violating codes of professional conduct and uprooting intellectual and moral power. Fear may have diminished courage, clouded common sense, and compromised personal integrity. At the same time that you were relying upon your internalized fear as the stimulus for whether or not you initiate constructive risk-taking, you may have also found it acceptable to operate in a diminished capacity. Activating those unwritten, impaired rules of conduct only serve as a substitute to mature development, replacing professionalism with blocked goals and blurring what constitutes right from wrong. This audit is to be used to fine-tune one's personal antennae. You are now being presented with an opportunity to rethink the defenses that you have employed—those deficient, self-protective barriers that have left you feeling unsatisfied and your family-run business impoverished. Your needs of now entail questioning the appropriateness of your coping mechanisms, which have infringed upon your professional development.

CHAPTER TWENTY-ONE:

A CRITICAL ANALYSIS– AUDITING YOUR FAMILY'S ESTRANGED ARRANGEMENT

Source: Expectations— Psychological Contracts Between Family Members

In one's hunger for recognition, one looks to self-define through the eyes of another. It is falsely believed that, "I can never be a winner by living up to my own expectations of myself. I need to live up to others' expectations to be recognized." Therefore, the journey to build self-esteem and to feel validated becomes misdirected. Looking outside of yourself for self-definition creates internalized fears—the catastrophizing and counter-productive "What if...then..." syndrome (introduced in Chapter Four). These fears are the motivators for the choices that we make in seeking recognition and shaping our behavior.

Expectation is a psychological contract between family members that is comprised of an attitude exchanged between individuals or the attitude of one toward self or others. It is collective unrealistic expectations which, when brought together, form a family or family-run business that is functioning devoid of psychological health. For each family, there are generally few sources, but the effects tend to multiply depending upon the number of family members impacted, their personality styles, and how each copes with on-going dissatisfaction.

Cause: Actions—Patterns of Behavior— Social Contracts Between Family Members

The emotional overtones reverberating within the family's work environment will reflect:

- One's ability to be trusting and trustworthy.
- One's willingness to risk involvement.
- One's feeling safe enough to disclose professional strengths, as well as professional weaknesses.
- One's desire to show initiative.
- One's desire to seek professional development.

A social contract between family members that fosters social well-being includes:

- Patterns of behavior that are mutually beneficial.
- Collaborative interdependence for the business' growth and goal achievement. This includes negotiating the use of power and authority, exercising cooperative intentions, and defining

conflicts in ways that bring enrichment through constructive resolution.
- A set of values that contribute to and promote well-being—values that one holds dear, consistently reflected in behavior.

A social contract between family members that erodes social well-being is behavior that seeks attention through control, dependency, or manipulation. This is a form of corruption. One is "buying love" through destructive means, since self-definition is purchased with the value one places on owning or possessing another, or the value one places on being owned or possessed. The choice to seek and earn attention through subversive channels is seen as more acceptable than receiving no attention at all. It is one's personal struggle for power. These actions, these patterns of behavior, cause problems. Do *not* interpret the *cause* of the problems as the *source* of the problems. The *cause* is not the *source*, merely the symptom.

For example, a member of a family-run business may choose not to speak to his co-workers about his concerns regarding on-going professionally inappropriate operating procedures. Rather, he goes home each evening and complains to his wife. This lack of open and straight-forward communication, which in turn gets redirected to an outside party, is not the source of the problem. It is merely a symptom of a broader problem of a family living within the confines of a closed relationship configuration. The family's rules and belief system (the *source*), which incorporates discouraging messages about the reper-cussions for openly expressing controversial thoughts and feelings, dictates the communication patterns which have *caused* this family member to withhold expressing his concerns to those directly impacted by and involved in the workplace dynamics. If you are not clear on this issue, you will be thrown off track and contaminate your final report.

- Symptoms such as control, dependency, and manipulation become a problem in themselves, even though they are taken on as a solution.
- Symptoms become forms of coping mechanisms (defenses) and, as such, shape behavior.
- Symptoms have the ability to generate low frustration tolerance, impatience, the seeking of immediate gratification, anger, procrastination, and retaliation.
- Symptoms are considered acts of defiance— defiance against the feeling of being cheated out of the emotional assurances that one is entitled to as an empowered psychologically and socially mature adult.

Effect: Internal and External Consequences of Cause— Adverse Outcomes—The Impact of Symptoms

The adverse outcome of internal consequences results in a betrayal, an abandonment of "self."

- Acting upon established defense mechanisms may be in direct conflict with the values that you associate with your own self-definition.
- Being deprived of a psychological separateness from your family leaves you anxious and experiencing self-doubt as to your ability to meet the challenge of mastering the developmental skill of differentiation.
- Having denied your basic human needs for so long

leaves you comfortable with the "procrastination trap," in which consistently putting things off becomes a habitual behavior.

The adverse outcome of external consequences results in a family divided.

- Unwritten but enforced rules of conduct create obstacles in how you direct your professional energy.
- Restrictiveness inhibits risk-taking for self-improvement and further imposes fear of disclosing awareness, concerns, and discontent.
- Underdeveloped interpersonal competence creates barriers to meaningful family relationships, as well as to your ability to define and master your family's true strengths.

The Ledger of L.O.V.E.:
Lost Opportunities Verified and Exposed

To **verify** is to establish the truth and attest to the reality of opportunities lost. To **expose** is to open to view those truths that are no longer shielded by busy-ness or protected by denial. To both verify and expose is to examine one's sense of responsibility, both to oneself, as well as to the business. The act of self-examination is a learning process that brings to discovery the potential for infinite possibilities that could lead to a corrective course of action. Once you embark upon this journey, you will eventually reach a turning point in which you recognize that the transition from sacrificing opportunities to embracing change is a positive and productive step. Engaging in the behavior of verifying and exposing lost opportunities is seizing the moment to identify existing toxins in order to cleanse the internal workings of the family-run business atmosphere.

Change cannot be negotiated until issues and positions have been clearly stated. This necessitates you determining whether or not your family is able to commit to a productive restructuring of the internal family-run business system, going beyond the limitations currently enforced which discourage the family's system of operation.

Determine whether or not your family is able to form and uphold a psychological contract between family members which, when mutually implemented, forms a family-run business in possession of psychological health (i.e., coercion in choice or action is absent; one is not bound by external controls, manipulations, or dependencies).

Assess the following:

- Are individual objectives in conflict?
- Can individual interests be merged?
- Is there an absence of trust?
- What motivations unite the members of your family-run business?
- What are family members' complementary abilities?
- Is the fragmentation too impaired for any reconstruction to take place in a business setting?

In Summation

At one time, it may have appeared meritorious that, as a family psychologically and socially divided, you were able to stay together. However, with reserves depleted, you are now unable to rebound from deprivations, perceived betrayals, and manipulations—this is the ultimate despair. No longer are you able to respond with any of the outward displays of enthusiasm needed to stir up activity; growth is inhibited, and the power to professionally endure feels destroyed.

Through this collective emotional underdevelopment, there has operated a group of unsophisticated individuals who have emotionally functioned more as children than as adults. In acting out unresolved family issues, no one has assumed the adult roles necessary to parent your family-run business. Your business is dependent upon your level of maturity and the degree of your collaborative effectiveness. With maturity and collaborative effectiveness compromised, the business gets placed in a "parentified role." A **parentified role** is an inverted relationship of looking to your business to fulfill your unmet emotional needs and your unrealistic expectations. It is an unsturdy and therefore unreliable foundation designated to influence and preserve family contacts, despite the lack of unity, joy, or purity of intent.

When you audit your family's business, you may experience the relief that comes with identifying those topics which carry a distinctive characteristic and concern. Identifying these issues may also produce anxiety. You may recognize the saddest truth of your family-run business' existence: being a part of each other's lives day-in and day-out, and yet never having built a foundation for genuine togethering, nurtured through the self-confidence that comes from one's own internal competence in conjunction with the encouragement, support, and co-operation of others. In other words, the focal points of a family-run business' internal standards are: (a) the need for all to be internally self-defined, acting upon those values associated with one's own self-definition; (b) the need to be firmly rooted in the blending of healthy self-identity with the freedom to be connected; and (c) the need to experience unifying business objectives which yield a power far beyond what each individual could achieve separately. Let us coin this concept, the focal points of a family-run business' internal standards, **Kin-Synergy**.

Table 7 reinforces the concept of Kin-Synergy by calling to your attention those characteristics that reflect a family divided, as well as those that reflect a family that is working on being united. As you review this table, you will be able to assess what portrait looks most like your own family. Those of you who have consistently identified with this chapter's theme may now find yourself at a crossroad. If this is in fact the case, you are only now realizing the depth of your emotional wounds. In order to perform in your business, your family has formed an estranged arrangement. Ask yourself: "Can we unite to turn our unnecessary pain into joy?" For some, the decision might be to go your own separate way professionally. This may be the most advantageous way for each family member to grow as an individual and for the family's wounds to heal. With clarification, one gains objectivity; from objectivity, one gains an understanding of solutions needed to assist one in going forward.

Table 7: A FAMILY PORTRAIT	
A Family Divided:	**A Family that is Working on Being United:**
• Deceives itself, hiding behind a pretense of being emotionally healthy	• Acknowledges limitations, dismantling the facade of "all is well"
• Feigns indifference to friendly working relationships and to genuine intimacy	• Yearns for friendly work relationships and for genuine intimacy
• Closes itself off to learning	• Opens itself up to learning
• Dreads change and becomes immobile	• Moves forward, willing to risk new ways of being
• Practices intolerance	• Practices tolerance
• Employs coercion and guilt	• Eliminates the use of coercion and guilt
• Engages in high-risk behaviors	• Engages in risk-worthy behaviors
• Violates workplace boundaries	• Assesses, institutes, and supports upholding professional boundaries
• Communicates in a discourteous and unrefined way	• Communicates in a courteous and refined way
• Discounts the value of an apology	• Makes amends without being prompted
• Closes itself off to constructive feedback	• Listens to constructive feedback
• Resists seeking professional intervention	• Seeks professional intervention

A CRITICAL ANALYSIS:
AUDITING OUR FAMILY'S ESTRANGED ARRANGEMENT

The following audit is a cognitive exercise. The objective is to encourage and promote clear thinking, to clarify goals, and to aid in deciding upon an appropriate and corrective course of action. Part One is designed for the audit-taker to conceptualize his or her family business involvement, keeping in mind that building a business is an evolutionary process. In this regard, one is prompted to specifically focus on three pivotal points in the family business history: (a) the decision to professionally come together to create a business; (b) the deterioration of the business (this does not necessarily mean financial deterioration) and the accompanying emotional impact; and (c) the subsequent realizations that come thereof. Part Two builds upon the encapsulated journey of Part One and is designed to prompt self-examination of a deeper level. The focus of this section is personalized to the individual audit-taker and concentrates on the psychological and social ramifications that have ensued as a result of this business venture. The format for both Parts One and Two is sentence completion—answering questions that will help you to assess not only the source, cause, effect, and L.O.V.E. (Lost Opportunities Verified and Exposed) of your family's working arrangement, but the degree of impairment. Is staying together a "go" or a "no?"

This assessment is not designed to be the sole factor in making such a life-altering decision. It is only to be used as a reference point to aid in being introspective, to enable you to acknowledge truths. This exercise also lends itself to a discussion among actively participating family-run business members, if this degree of risk-taking (to self-disclose and acknowledge issues) is an avenue that you choose to explore.

Directions: On a separate piece of paper, write out your answers to these sentence completions, being as specific as you can in your wording, avoiding vagueness. Using descriptive words gives a pin-point focus to what you have instinctively been aware of but were resistant to dispute. Doing so now is a step toward growth, in spite of any accompanying discomforts.

PART ONE

Source: Expectations
1. As a family, our "voiced" reasons for initially coming together were...
2. My own "voiced" reasons for joining my family in business were...
3. I now believe that our "unvoiced" (hidden) expectations of initially coming together—our "Love For Sale" contract—were characterized by the conditional fulfillment of...

Cause: Actions Resulting from our Expectations
4. I am aware of how we have degenerated as a family in business, as evidenced by...
5. I am also aware of my own degeneration, as evidenced by my unexpressed feelings of...
6. This is expressed in my behaviors through...

Effect: Internal and External Impacts of Cause
7. As a family, we are currently in an emotional state of...
8. I, personally speaking, am currently in an emotional state of...
9. If I decide to go my own way, I need to...
10. For us to stay together, we would need to...

11. The greatest risk of staying together is...

12. The greatest risk of breaking up is...

L.O.V.E.: Lost Opportunities Verified and Exposed

13. As a family, we lost the opportunity to...

14. As an individual, I lost the opportunity to...

15. If we choose to stay together as a family in business, we can work toward reclaiming these opportunities by...

16. Whether or not we choose to stay together as a family in business, we need to work toward reclaiming...

PART TWO

Source: Expectations

17. I live up to the expectations of (name of individual)...

18. I do this by (your behavior)...

19. I interpret his/her expectations to be (name the perceived expectations)...

20. If I don't live up to these expectations, my fear is (write out what you perceive as your fear)...

21. The result of this fear could be...

** (Repeat numbers 17 through 21 in order to identify and assess the perceived expectations of *each* family member who works with you in the family business.)

22. My own expectations of my family members who participate with me in this family-run business are...

Cause: Actions

Because of these "expectations," I took on maladaptive patterns of behavior as self-protective defense mechanisms. I now realize that I have contributed to our family's current status in the following ways:

23. When I participate in a restrictive relationship, my intent is to...

24. I do this in the following ways (identify your actions)...
25. Through this control style, I defend myself against my fear of...
26. When I participate in a demanding relationship, my intent is to...
27. I do this in the following ways (identify your actions)...
28. Through this control style, I defend myself against my fear of...
29. When I participate in an oppressive relationship, my intent is to...
30. I do this in the following ways (identify your actions)...
31. Through this control style, I defend myself against my fear of...

Effect: Adverse Outcomes

32. Up until this point, my preferred coping style has negatively impacted my functioning as a team player by...
33. Up until this point, my preferred coping style has negatively impacted my own work-related responsibilities by me focusing my energies on...
34. I should be focusing my energies instead on...
35. Up until this point, my preferred coping style has negatively impacted my psychological development by...
36. Up until this point, my preferred coping style has negatively impacted my professional development by...

L.O.V.E.: Lost Opportunities Verified and Exposed

37. As a member of my family's business, I threw away the opportunity of...
38. In so doing, I have devalued myself by...
39. Our family-run business has suffered by...
40. Genuine loving behavior was penalized through...

PART FOUR:

BECOMING DEVELOPABLE– WORKING OUT THE POSSIBILITIES

CHAPTER TWENTY-TWO:

RECOVERING FROM DESTRUCTIVE ENERGY

Destructive energy is a killer of growth. It is now time to create an atmosphere conducive to and permissible for members of a family-run business to seek opportunities for development. Years of living and working in a closed family system has sabotaged individuation through laborious emotional bondage, characterized by toilsome effort directed toward seeking recognition and validation with little or no personal gratification.

Professional competence for a family-run business encapsulates much more than that of a business whose leadership and employee status are not family-run and operated. The challenge of identifying and addressing whether or not family members in business are connected by laborious emotional bondage or by genuine bonding is essential for changing how one thinks about and runs a family-run business. The family operating in a disordered fashion is devalued; this leaves not only the individual members devalued, but the business as well. Choosing to maintain these maladaptive functions is choosing to be held hostage by one's fears.

Rather than *bonding* to one's family, one is volunteering to be in *bondage*. To **bond** is to embrace. It is a relationship that is secure in the individuation of its participants, encouraging their differentiation. A relationship held in **bondage** is *not* one that is secure in the individuation of its participants, nor does it encourage this differentiation. It is an attempt to control by clinging to patterns of behavior that only serve to compromise family unity and professional integrity. The belief that one does not have choice—fearing abandonment or rejection if one does not comply with expected family rules and roles—can leave one immobilized, not trusting oneself to make healthy, appropriate lifestyle changes.

This text has outlined a comprehensive and focused perspective on family-run business dynamics. The intent is to clarify the limitations under which family members operate. For a family to thrive, it is essential to realize the conditions that need to be satisfied by each member. As a visual aid, it would be beneficial and suitable to formulate a written description of how each member's individual responsibilities directly correspond to those responsibilities assigned to the rest of the team. This would promote an enhanced awareness of the interdependence of the work system. This task also reinforces how a family's work system competence includes a social structure that can only be oriented toward the forward movement of its members. Forward movement can be appraised by: (a) a reliable, built-in monitoring system for assessing the organization's on-going business practices; and (b) resilience in realigning when the team loses sight of priorities. In its broadest sense, this approach reinforces the commitment that each player has to nurturing his or her own professional self-worth and how one's perceived value impacts the business' overall well-being. In a family-run business, each member shares the responsibility of broadening the family's psychological and social capabilities in order for all to reap the financial and emotional rewards.

Neglecting to assess the overall system (failing to weigh the relevant business practices that are praiseworthy against unsatisfactory business practices that are detrimental and that do not ensure future benefits) increases the likelihood for long-term negative conse-quences that are emotionally painful. This implies complications—complications that result in family-run business policies which are inappropriate to a business setting. It also can result in individual family members being incompatible with their assigned responsibilities, which directly corresponds to problems with accountability. Ask yourself: in the assigning of specific functions, is each member constructing a career with professional codes of conduct directed toward goals that befit sound business practices?

Being **resilient** is having the ability to recover from the misfortunes of having participated in a disordered family-run business environment. It is giving oneself permission to dismantle the aftereffects of destructive energies—negative characteristics that have diminished the ability to effectively serve both the personal and professional components that make up a family-run business. Being resilient is empowering. It is a function of mental health. Resilience carries with it four distinct attributes, all surrounding **elimination**—ridding oneself of language or behavior that debilitates ego strength and hinders self-confidence and determination. These four attributes are: (a) eliminating one's view of self as a victim; (b) eliminating denial; (c) eliminating self-pity; and (d) eliminating polarities of tolerance.

Eliminating One's View of Self as a Victim

Viewing oneself as a victim results in the attitude that one is at the mercy of outside forces that are committed to destroying one's freedom of self-expression. Always perceiving oneself on the threshold of danger or misfortune carries a mentality which promotes polarized thinking with little room for middle ground, thus leading to extreme choices in behavior. One can choose to take on a *passive* attitude—giving in to the hopelessness of it all; acting needy, helpless, or dependent; seeking to be rescued from the dis-eases that accompany developing as an adult. Or one can choose to take on an *aggressive* attitude—acting out the idea that you must "victimize others before they can victimize you." The anti-social behavior of bullying manifests in habitual cruelty (through an approach of abusive language and/or behavior) used to threaten, intimidate, discredit, and undermine others. The underlying intent is to gain a position of power and to eliminate one's own feeling of powerlessness by causing pain to another. This is a short term pay-off for getting your own way. It is an uninhibited harshness without regard for consequences. It could also include a manner which displays arrogance, in which one exaggerates one's worth or importance (to one's business and/or to one's family) with intent to enhance a feeling of victimization or powerlessness in others.

210

Behaviors that push people away and undermine mutuality are not a solution to solving internal or interpersonal conflicts. Both polarities—passive and aggressive approaches—to viewing oneself as a victim are merely ways of living up to one's developmental weaknesses and embracing the enemy within. Although employing a victim mentality is initially incorporated as an adaptive function to self-protect, in the long run, it brings about complications, adding to the complexities that already exist. It is betraying one's potential, sacrificing one's self-respect on the altar of recognition hunger. Self-induced emotional imprisonment causes an alienation from comfort. It behooves one to consider eliminating this perspective of seeing oneself as a victim, of living with the mentality of "me versus them." By eliminating this self-view, you can realign the reality of what actually is with the reality of what could be. You can set standards and abide by the realistic appraisal of how you go about choosing to be responsible for your role in your family-run business. It is invigorating to use methods that bring out one's strengths rather than one's weaknesses. A family business in possession of psychological and social fitness is a business that prospers.

Eliminating Denial

One who sees oneself as a victim looks outside of oneself for the cause of his or her discomfort. With maturity comes taking on the responsibility for looking inside of oneself to find the causes of one's discomfort. Facing facts and owning truths is dealing with denial. Of course, this implies changing patterns of habit. Learn the self-discipline necessary to achieve emotional growth, and from that will come the ability for the family to be truly united.

Dealing with denial through changing patterns of habit leaves one feeling vulnerable, exposed, and unprotected. It is natural to ask, "Can I, as a member of my family, withstand the uncertainty that comes with taking a chance?" This chance is to jump-start arrested growth. With new-found growth comes opportunity. As discussed in Chapter Nineteen, one opportunity may result in the all too vivid recognition that, if as a collective professional unit you personally are unable to experience growth, then going your own separate way is appropriate. This may be the only way to salvage your connection to the family unit.

Consider these essential and relevant elements which collectively constitute the task to be performed:

- Reassess personal and professional limitations. Fine-tune your psychological antenna to no longer focus on what you cannot change, but on what you *can* change. You have choices.
- Stop denying your own personal power. A victim mentality only serves to fuel non-affirming thought patterns that give strength to words and phrases like "can't," "if only," "yes, but," and "if it weren't for...."
- Resistance to owning the facts leaves you emotionally blinded; with clarity compromised, responsible decision-making is jeopardized.
- Acknowledge the limitations that you encounter, as well as the setbacks and the difficulties in developing and applying new behavioral skills. This is of benefit in assessing which situations are repairable and which are irreparable so that you can put your focus where you will be most effective. Avoidance of being discriminating is also self-destructive behavior and can drain you of confidence and energy.

- Do not believe that insight or emotional catharsis is sufficient in and of itself to repair or cure dis-ease. To believe so is an indication of denying the energy and commitment of time necessary for effective behavioral change to result.
- To accept on-going assurances of change from family-run business members without any evidence in actual professional performance behavior is to maintain denial of reality and perpetuate the existing damage to self and others.

Eliminating Self-Pity

Being drained of confidence and energy leads one to self-pity. When you pity yourself, you are a victim of your own negativity. When environmental cues have you interpreting negativity as being effective, negativity becomes aggressively injurious; it has a tendency to infiltrate your core and relentlessly cause deterioration in your outlook. This does not mean that you blatantly deny the grief that comes with actual deprivation and loss, but you cannot allow your deprivations and your losses to control you. If you accept the deprivations and losses of the past to be controlling influences in the present, your family's business future for potential growth and healing will drown in collective self-pity.

Eliminating self-pity incorporates the following:

- Stop rationalizing the weaknesses in yourself to make the unacceptable acceptable.
- Release the hurts of the past that, until now, have hindered you from empowering yourself.
- Develop a sense of self-worth, eliminating distortions that have become incorporated into your

213

belief system as "truth."

- Eliminate the internalized questioning of, "When is it my turn to be taken care of? Why isn't someone stepping in to take care of me?" This corrupts your sense of responsibility to yourself.
- Identify when you are manipulating. Self-pity has a cumulative effect. You don't just pity yourself, you invest in behaviors to guarantee that others will pity, protect, and rescue you from taking responsibility for yourself.
- Acknowledge those self-protective behaviors that keep you emotionally and socially distant.
- Recognize when you are interpreting your sorrow as stemming from another's disloyalty. This reasoning escalates self-pity into the domain of blame, which falsely releases you from taking responsibility for yourself. Hence, you stay emotionally stuck.

Eliminating Polarities of Tolerance

The polarities of tolerance demand an exploration of attitudes. One extreme is *having a high tolerance for inappropriate behaviors*. Behavior is inappropriate when it socially deviates from professional codes of conduct and standard operating procedures. Allowing such behavior brings complications to the dual relationship of family members who are incorporated into the family-run business organization. To be successful, a family-run business must assign a specific function to each participating member, a function which serves to complete the overall operational equation in a favorable way.

The other extreme is *intolerance*. This behavior is evidenced by having a personality that does not accept beliefs or practices which differ from or conflict with one's own. When one is unwilling to incorporate the perspectives and habits of others (despite a work culture that provides for a range of variation where all can still grow and thrive), this provocative behavior can be interpreted as an expression of aggression. An intolerant person stubbornly exercises, free of guilt, his or her individual choice to the detriment of a collaborative work environment.

Being intolerant of others, as well as having a high tolerance for inappropriate behaviors, sabotages team building. To promote team building, members need to clarify their existing and potential contributions to the team. The intolerant need to widen their views of others' abilities and valued qualities. Those with high tolerance for inappropriate behavior (accepting practices which are unacceptable and unproductive to a business' environment) need to examine and process their motivations for their displaced loyalty.

The impact of these extremes diminishes overall operational effectiveness and true leadership. What is generated in place of effectiveness is a maladaptive group of individuals who need to readjust their perceptions of their assigned roles. Taking corrective action to overcome polarities of tolerance will require you to:

- Redefine collaborative behavior.
- Diagnose, through observation, your business' current style of functioning.
- Devise strategies for effective change—change which is relevant to the family-run business developing as a professional organization.
- Define performance in terms that legitimately profile a business that is committed to promoting

personal empowerment, in which your individual tasks are interdependent upon group tasks.
• Demonstrate a philosophy which encourages reluctant participants to contribute.

In Summation

Elimination of the victimization of self and others, denial, self-pity, and polarities of tolerance enables you to let go of old patterns that disable healing. Eliminate elements that erode and corrupt your ability to act upon healthy functional change. Make the switch from ineptness to adeptness; turn inadequacies into adequacies, the uncomfortable into the comfortable. Become developable. Being **developable** means: (a) promoting the psychological and social growth of a family-run business; (b) providing more opportunity for effective use of professionalism; (c) causing change to unfold and gradually acquiring the benefits thereof; and (d) experiencing a natural process of differentiation and connectedness. *The destructive lengths that a family-run business will undergo to maintain family contact have been underestimated.*

Identify desirable patterns of behavior that will create a professional environment conducive to restoring social stability—in other words, a healthy climate of interaction. Begin to see the effects of your own behavior on others. A family who invests in demonstrating its powerlessness as a family in business is demeaning the business' very existence. These kinds of negative behaviors have not only been tolerated, but endorsed. A family comprised of disordered individuals believes that receiving negative attention is better than receiving no attention at all. This collective ultimate fear is what generates the emotional bondage. As a result, the family continues to engage in destructive behaviors in order to self-confirm. Unfortunately, this philosophy will not help to create a family accomplished, a family united. Individuals need to work on setting boundaries for their own behavior, while the business sets and enforces professional standards of operating. To achieve professionally as a family, one is required to learn **pro-social behavior**: (a) standards of practice that depict collaboration; (b) interventions that are effective by demonstrating power through recognition of professional procedure and conduct; and (c) voluntarily amending roles when warranted to generate and accelerate the prosperous development of "growing emotionally" as a family. When a family is rightfully concerned with the performance of its principal players, it begins to engage in profit-seeking through placing a value on defining professional competence and aligning it with social competence. Behavior that is responsive to aligning the social with the professional is a style of functioning that expresses being in control through the language of maturity. The identification of these practical alternatives leads to exploration of self and new territory for a family in development.

Table 8 depicts the views of families who are learning the values of professional identity and accountability.

Table 8:
PROFESSIONAL IDENTITY AND ACCOUNTABILITY— A FRESH PERSPECTIVE

- The family-run business is a family redefining itself.

- The family-run business provides the opportunity for new roles to emerge within a supportive framework—roles which are appropriate to a professional business setting.

- The expression of opinions and the sharing of feelings is respected.

- Developing a climate of trust is an important element in the building of a cohesive professional work environment.

- The psychological and social well-being of a family is essential for building a business' economic foundation.

- Engaging in an optimum level of functioning is essential to group cohesiveness.

- An individual's professional and personal growth and development is a valued step in achieving a family-run business that is accomplished.

- Problem-solving is a creative process, in which resolution is approached in an uncomplicated manner, accompanied by cooperative behaviors that lead to the attainment of organizational goals.

- Neglecting specific areas of operation, as evidenced by the team's malfunctioning, is an aspect of abuse.

- Social needs, such as privacy rights, allocation of personal space, and independence in carrying out one's job description, are important to the business experience.

- Being divided represents anti-growth.

- Being united is a measurement of a family's fitness—being fit to be together in business.

CHAPTER TWENTY-THREE:

GETTING DOWN TO BUSINESS

It's All Perspective

Undertaking a process of resocialization is an art, a creative adventure. For some families in business who are committed to staying in business, this will require a radical change. Non-committed attitudes and superficial attempts at self-discipline will only serve to further deteriorate those areas of functioning which are already impaired. The goal is to cultivate a family-run business work environment that is markedly distinguishable from one's initial "labor-of-bondage." The potential for accomplishing this is dependent upon a family's willingness to risk investing in the reorganization of social and professional behaviors. The beneficiaries of this professional undertaking will receive the proceeds of their acts of well-being: a deep sense of satisfaction through the achievement of bonding.

When clear, sensible, distinguishable resolutions are being achieved, they are recognizable to the observing eye and thoughtful mind. A united determination constitutes a movement toward that which is noteworthy and which represents an unmistakable difference between prior family-run business interaction and present attentiveness. This uniformity, this existing wholeness, will indeed serve to revitalize the family-run business' social energy and contribute to the resilience of the family's emotional spirit.

Effort is directed at identifying the opportunities to develop interpersonal and professional family relationships and to move beyond difficulties that seem incapable of resolution. It is a test of one's ability to simultaneously co-exist with diverse and oftentimes adversarial emotions. It is an achievement representing endurance, courage, and strength of mind when one is able to keep separate these powerful contradictory feelings and incompatible attitudes while extending considerable attention befitting each. It implies a family of individuals who are not opposed or indifferent to the mandatory devotion needed to overcome outmoded social-order and policy.

Honor the Struggle for Progress

Progress, the moving forward to a more advanced stage of interpersonal family-run business development, will be a gradual journey. Progress is not intended to be a roller coaster ride of ups-and-downs and dangerous curves. One wants to avoid the heartbreak of another intense emotional encounter—encounters that have been all too familiar, and therefore comforting in an uncomfortable way. Skills are not always easy to master when one begins to delve into the complexities that make up the family-run business experience. Up to this point, the work situation has been devoid of the necessary support systems. Initially, it is normal for family-run business members to struggle when approaching situations in an unfamiliar way. One feels vulnerable when charting new territory. Given constructive intent and appropriate application, one will elicit a more desired response, even though new behavior has not been perfected. Regardless of the gratification of applying a new, healthier behavior and receiving a desired response, one still feels at a disadvantage when setting aside tried-and-true performance styles. New role behavior, while healthier, is still not the well-acquainted, closely intimate style of behavior one activated in response to situation-specific events of the past. In this transition of adapting to and owning new behavior, one may feel an increased vulnerability to being victimized by those family members whose response or intentions one still does not trust. This skepticism may be prevalent but, hopefully, temporary. Negative feelings of skepticism (even if appropriate) have the ability to control one's choice of response, leaving one reticent to change and thus unable to move forward.

There are benefits to enlisting in the struggle for progress. When one is committed to being an active participant, not merely a sideline observer, advancements can be made and outdated behaviors can change. The experience of change starts to remove the mystery of change; constructive behavior is accorded the respect and validation it deserves. If everyone involved remains invested in how best to contribute to addressing the central issues, enrichment will be gained. No one person is capable of making a genuinely positive and lasting impact alone. Attitude does affect outcome. Collective accountability will influence not only emotional well-being, but work performance as well. When cooperation is generated, resistance is modified and a balanced perspective is able to be established.

There are other risks in making advancements in the name of progress. Revamping inappropriate and unwanted systems of operating inspires individuals to expand their previously perceived limits of change. Feeling motivated by riding high on the course of a healthier business lifestyle, personal lifestyle changes begin to occur with the intent to further enhance one's commitment to change. One no longer wants to uphold an ill-suited family role or to victimize oneself. The emphasis is on long-term change— a solidified resocialization of the family *and* the family in business. The unbalanced, out-of-focus, emotionally restrictive individual can now become a balanced visionary, free to attain mastery not only in family-run business pursuits, but in one's non-work-related relationships as well. At first, this makes the "new and improved" individual(s) appear unpredictable. In the course of change, the healthier are no longer able to be manipulated as they once were, nor do they wish to manipulate. This brings conflicted emotions for those who experience a slower change in themselves and who struggle with their commitment and discipline. There may be gladness for a loved-one who is psychologically and socially prospering; there also may be feelings of frustration. Old ways of emotionally relating no longer apply. So the ante is raised and the choice is to also grow or to go.

Anticipate the tendency toward setbacks. This is to be expected and can be defined as simply *deconstructing advancements*. Setbacks are low points, which are evidenced when:

- Issues go unspoken.
- Solutions are inferred, but not specified.
- Investment in growth is random and not targeted to the needs of now.
- Truth is modified.
- Conformity is used not to unite for the resocialization process, but to return to one's dis-eased relationships.

When emotional dynamics fluctuate, commitment can be lax. This could be due in part to a disbelief in the family's ability to change and in part to unrealistic expectations of what change offers. You need to be clear on what your role is in the progression of change. Identify how you want to see yourself after having made the changes necessary to reach the desired vision. Do not focus energy primarily on the forward movement of others, letting your own energy lag behind. There need to be collective goals as well as individual goals. All goals need to be specific, realistic, measurable, attainable, and based on needs of now. (*Not* needs of the past—needs of now!) It is an absolute necessity that goals be appropriate to your family's business situation. Otherwise, you are only adding to low morale and inviting chaotic, ineffective behavior. Living by destructive defense mechanisms may have become normal operating procedure, but *normal does not necessarily mean healthy.*

Create Meaning by Nourishing Morale

Morale can be beneficial or detrimental to productivity. Low morale can decrease one's investment in wanting to be an active participant in the process of moving forward to a satisfying change. A struggling, unhealthy family-run business environment can de-motivate. Therefore, morale in a family-run business becomes an issue of the heart. While motivation comes from within, there are those attitudes unique to a family-run business which can contribute to de-motivation. This strongly influences morale.

Nourishing morale should not be thought of as a single event, a passing fad, or a "let's humor them" attitude. It is creating a comfortable, workable environment that not only finds enthusiasm for dismantling destructive energy, but also finds joy in freeing inhibited energy. Nourishing morale is two-fold: the elimination of feelings that burden the spirit, and the expression of an attitude that encourages goodwill. It is vital to affirm each other's dedication to this creative adventure—an adventure comprised of advancements and setbacks. The willingness to commit to this undertaking with all of its unknowns and risks is to venture on a remarkable journey.

Affirming each other allows participants to feel secure in the knowledge that they are now part of a family-run business process. This process requires the necessary discipline to nurture a stylized support system which will give pleasure in areas where once there was none. This spirit of goodwill is a built-in damage control, protecting the individual team member's path of growth. This spirit is also a responsive and sensitive way to lend emotional support to another's growth, even when his or her growth may challenge or collide with your own. It is a vehicle for practicing tolerance for self and others.

It's an Issue of Heart

Giving yourself permission to directly confront your risk-related issues shows not only courage, but a temperament that is generous of spirit. To attack the virus of anti-growth is to begin to heal the damage that took years to develop. This damage cannot be cured merely by openly acknowledging a healing intent, nor simply by reading this book. The healing begins with *action*.

While confrontational and possibly painful, consider this text to be your family's first booster shot: a vaccine to encourage a collaborative developmental process, an immunizing agent whose primary objective is to reinforce one's identification with specific recurring themes. Through openly acknowledging this identification, one can set upon a course to recover from conditions that have contributed to a family's lack of psychological and social health. Launch your campaign, make a commitment, kindle the process of maturing, and establish the "new-and-improved" family-run business. Consistently performing in a socially and professionally appropriate manner is not only healthy, it is contagious. The enthusiasm of experiencing maturity spreads to others. The family experiencing itself as a constructive, functional workplace team can finally tap into its potential.

Let your business become an instrument of power, not by outward appearances to the public, but by an internal knowledge enriched by consistency in professional behavior. Each member will carry the distinction of being part of something special and being proud to contribute to one's own "family-esteem." It would be a sad testimony at the end of one's productive years (years which were meant to yield benefits, profits, and the satisfaction of wants) to have been part of a family that professed unity but conformed to distorted ideals of what constituted "a professional family." If there is to be conformity, let it be a conformity born out of the self-identity that comes from maturity. Let there be a mutual commitment by all to eliminate negative precepts, to broaden the scope of pre-existing codes of conduct, and to employ stronger principles which shape functional discipline. Eliminate collective deprivations that undermine self-identity and discourage healthy connectedness. Discard the busy-ness and give yourself permission to *get down to the business of growing emotionally.*

CHAPTER TWENTY-FOUR:

TO BE–
OR NOT TO BE–
ACCOMPLISHED

This final chapter is structured around the design of acronyms. An **acronym** is a word that is formed from the initial letters of other selective words. When these selective words are grouped together in a particular order, a message is directly conceived. This chapter's message is one which focuses on two key concepts addressed throughout this text. The first key concept is the maturation process of psychological and social growth. To *grow emotionally* entails a systematic series of actions directed toward some end. That end is the second key concept that this text puts forth— that of a family-run business standing *united*. To believe in, commit to, and aim for this developmental process of becoming is a family-run business' ultimate journey—the journey of becoming accomplished.

G Garden
R Rally
O Overturn
W Warm Up

E Encourage
M Monitor
O Optimize
T Translate
I Initiate
O Organize
N Negotiate
A Assert
L Learn
L Liberate
Y Yield

Garden: Deserts are made into gardens by pioneers who take chances on uncertain outcomes. There are no guarantees when you risk. Stakes are virtually always high when you opt to develop unfertilized soil. Now is the time to plant sound principles and cultivate professional strategies. Rules have to be changed. There may be setbacks and losses, but the object is to work the soil so as to maximize the opportunity to germinate a diverse garden of suitable professionals who share a common ground.

Rally: This is a call to action for a common purpose—coming together to rebuild the initial foundation of your business. To encourage group enthusiasm, you must exemplify qualities that move people forward—qualities that carry dignity, elevate business operations, increase the maturity of the business' participants, and carry a heightened sense of personal responsibility by all.

This is the opportunity to justify the business' psychological and social existence in healthy, meaningful terms.

Overturn: Having previously enshrined mediocrity, it is now time to overturn that which was emotionally disturbing and right the wrongs. To take this higher position, you must not only offer your willingness and readiness to begin the process, but you must make yourself available as well. Overturn the proposition that "love is for sale." Productivity, responsibly executed, is what is now being sold.

Warm Up: The undertaking to repair or replace defective family dynamics requires extra-ordinary personal power. It is beneficial to create healing psychological tactics in which you warm up to releasing your untapped potential and hidden assets. Practice affirming yourself, demonstrate a positive attitude within, and challenge internal destroyers of confidence. Visualize yourself as a winner, no matter what lies ahead for the business. Warm up to the idea that you can depend upon yourself to do what is honorable and professional. Warm up to allowing yourself to experience a surge of emotions; give voice to those feelings that need to be heard. Warm up to initiating discussions associated with and relevant to growing as a family. Warm up to the possibility of joining in close association with a family member who has previously been seen as uncooperative in business relations. Warm up to being an active participant in your own professional growth. Enjoy the challenge.

Encourage: Endorse clear thinking. This assists in promoting a realistic appraisal of events and gives strength to your ability to let go of beliefs that are sabotaging in nature.

Monitor: Attentively watch your resistance to situational change. Be sure to discipline yourself in accurately discerning those aspects of change that cannot be compromised with those that can. Regulate unnecessary apprehension and patterns of behavior that are prone to undermine performance.

Optimize: Make effective use of all opportunities which are directed toward your professional and emotional growth. Maximize the value of each lesson for the most favorable outcome. Be optimistic.

Translate: It is time to convert your risk-worthy desires into action. Apply newly learned ways of living that arouse a state of self-satisfaction. Transform self-sabotaging performance traits into growth-producing attributes.

Initiate: Be a learned leader. Model your conduct to reflect someone who: (a) displays refined communication skills; (b) collaborates with colleagues when making decisions that will ultimately impact the team; and (c) appropriately pursues solutions to questionable and difficult issues. Set an example as an individual who values differentiation, while at the same time responsibly represents the interests of the business.

Organize: Lay the foundation for a family work environment that embraces team building and displays collaborative interdependence. Give structure to operating procedures that will enhance task performance while enlisting co-operative participation.

Negotiate: Professionally speaking, come to terms with your own unmet needs. According to circumstances, adjust that which is adjustable—without neglecting to show consideration for the whole. Transact the discussions on these issues in a satisfactory manner, where all concerned feel heard, understood, and respected.

Assert: Declare your views with self-assurance. Support your right to express both positive and negative feelings. In all confrontations, maintain your dignity and the dignity of others.

Learn:	Pursue the acquisition of knowledge. To be learned is to be acquainted with truth. Expose yourself to new experiences. Advocate being well-informed. Growth connects you to the process of acquiring skills, modifying behaviors through practice, and achieving mastery of your life.

Liberate:	Free yourself from social constraints arising from unrealistic role expectations and rules that are inclined to prevent psychological and social well-being. Release others who you may be holding in emotional bondage—those who have been internally bound by control, dependency, or manipulation.

Yield:	Investing in the process of good orderly direction relinquishes resistance, fear, anger, and low self-esteem thinking. Cultivating positive energy releases destructive energy. This systematic series of actions gives rise to a superior power that does not require surrendering your individuality to your enemy within—the negative self-talk that opposes growth and resists the striving toward self-actualization. Making the effort to achieve your full potential represents maturity. Maturity will be the fruit of your labor.

AFFIRMATION: In giving myself permission to "Grow Emotionally," I have gained perspective. What has been done cannot be undone. I have achieved an inner strength when I let go of my regret and self-pity. In my maturity, I am now open to receive the richness that comes from mastering being "United."

U Unlock
N Name
I Intermingle
T Trust
E Expand
D Dream

Unlock: Furnishing yourself with the key that will free you from the restraints and restrictions that have previously hindered your psychological and social development will invariably lead you toward becoming an effective and valuable team player. You will no longer need to pretend to get along, to have a positive attitude, or to know all of the answers. Unlocking your internal sources of power will prompt you to discard pretenses that are no longer needed.

Name: List and rank those qualities that distinguish your family as "divided" and as "united." In addressing the divided aspects of your business, factually specify what approach you would prescribe to remedy this dis-eased condition. Be sure to utilize those strengths that your family business members currently possess that will assist in managing your "treatment" process (Table 7, page 199, listed under the "United" column). What would it look like if your business were to triumph?

Intermingle: Sometimes the most unlikely ingredients meld together, thus creating a delightful surprise. What were once considered separate entities of a business may unite to be a vital source of power. Blending different opinions and merging varied approaches may lead to unlimited possibilities. The intermingling of the seemingly unrelated may produce a high yield on your emotional investment.

Trust: Be assured that the commitment to grow emotionally—to take responsibility for your own psychological and social well-being—will benefit all concerned. Growth is

232

not exact; it does not strictly conform to a standard pattern. Growth entails being open to new ideas and educating yourself in areas that will encourage self-expression. Growth embraces opportunities for change. Believe and trust in this process, since being intimately connected and committed to this journey is a prerequisite for a family in business together.

Expand: Anticipate the best possible outcome. In growing emotionally, you (as an individual separate from your family) fulfill an essential function and a deep-rooted desire. When you open up your capacity for change, you extend the parameters of your being. When each family member participates in his or her own intrapersonal venture, the business as a whole has a greater potential to function in harmony—collectively as one.

Dream: Imagine your family living and working united. Imagine your family devoted to the codes of conduct that exhibit good, orderly direction. Imagine holding yourself in esteem and, through this underlying quality, propelling yourself toward individuation—the ultimate fulfillment of recognition hunger. Imagine seeing *yourself* as a prize. New possibilities await. Venture forth.

AFFIRMATION: In giving myself permission to master being "United," I am applying my new-found knowledge, skills, and personal power. I have gained a thorough understanding of the distinction between the family's "business-of-living" and the family's "living-of-business." I now display interpersonal competence in my professional performance. I encourage and support collaborative interdependence and the empowerment of my family members to work on their own professional self health-care. I now possess a vitality of spirit. *I am accomplished.*

REFERENCES

Ansbacher, H. L., & Ansbacher, R. R. (Eds.). (1964). The individual psychology of Alfred Adler: A systematic presentation in selections from his writings. New York: Harper & Row, Inc.

Berne, E. (1964). Games people play. New York: Random House.

Bowen, M. (1994). Family therapy in clinical practice. (4th edition). Northvale, NJ: Jason Aronson.

Bowlby, J. (1988). A secure base: Parent-child attachment and healthy human development. U.S.A.: Basic Books, Inc.

Bradshaw, J. (1988). Bradshaw on: The family. Pompano Beach, FL: Health Communications, Inc.

Dreikurs, R. (1964). Children: The challenge. New York: Hawthorn Books, Inc.

Ellis, A. (1962). Reason and emotion in psychotherapy. New York: Lyle Stuart.

Ellis. A., & Becker, I. M. (1982). A guide to personal happiness. North Hollywood, CA: Wilshire Book Company.

Fagen, J., & Shepherd, I. L. (Eds.). (1970). <u>Frederick S. Perls, "Four Lectures," Gestalt theory now.</u> Palo Alto, CA: Science and Behavioral Books, Inc.

Guerin, P. J., Jr., Fogarty, T. F., Fay, L. F., & Kautto, J. G. (1996). <u>Working with relationship triangles: The one-two-three of psychotherapy.</u> New York: The Guilford Press.

Love, P. (1990). <u>The emotional incest syndrome: What to do when a parent's love rules your life.</u> New York: Bantam Books.

McGoldrick, M., & Gerson, R. (1985). <u>Genograms in family assessment.</u> New York: W. W. Norton & Company.

Merriam-Webster, Inc. (1984). <u>Webster's ninth new collegiate dictionary.</u> Springfield, MA: Author.

Powell, J. (1969). <u>Why am I afraid to tell you who I am?</u> Allen, TX: Argus Communications.

Prather, H. (1970). <u>Notes to myself.</u> Moab, UT: Real People Press.

Ryan, R. M., & Lynch, J. H. (1989). Emotional autonomy versus detachment: Revisiting the vicissitudes of adolescence and young adulthood. <u>Child Development, 60,</u> 340-356.

Satir, V. (1972). <u>Peoplemaking.</u> Palo Alto, CA: Science and Behavior Books, Inc.

GLOSSARY

Accomplishment — the achievement of psychological and social maturity which is derived from the private and professional interactions of a family, influenced by relational roles. A family already in harmony (individuals who are not confused, conflicted, and/or confined by their thoughts, feelings, and behaviors), or a family that is able to overcome the afore-mentioned social discomforts and emotional distress, will emerge to create a work environment that is harmonious. One is free to find one's own balance of expressing healthy differentness with a blend of healthy connectedness.

Addiction — continued investment in the repetition of destructive behavior through the chronic misuse of an activity, despite negative consequences. Negative consequences manifest in such areas of one's life as physical, psychological, social, financial, and legal problems.

Attachment behavior — the development of a specific social attachment, first organized in early child-hood development as a function attributed to that of protection. This attribute develops over time and is influenced by satisfying or unsatisfying interactions with key people in a child's environ-ment. Parental characteristics and child-rearing practices strongly influence the consequences of attachment (secure or anxious) for the social and emotional development of the evolving individual, in response to forming other significant intimate relationships.

Belief system — can be constructive and serve to encourage and promote rational and reasonable interpretations of events, giving one the ability to view oneself and others realistically and accurately. Or, a belief system can be destructive and serve to discourage and promote irrational and unreasonable interpretations of events, causing oneself and others to be viewed unrealistically and inaccurately. A constructive belief system supports looking at facts and truths. A destructive belief system has a tendency to exaggerate and distort the facts.

Bondage — a family that is not emotionally mature will not possess the ability to encourage its individual members to be distinct in personhood. The temptation will be to control—by clinging to patterns of behavior that only serve to compromise family unity and a family-run business' professional integrity. This emotional confinement is influenced by the belief that one does not have choice. One is threatened by the fear of abandonment or rejection if one does not comply with expected family rules and roles. The strength of this conviction—influenced by the interpretation one has given to past experiences—can leave one immobilized, not trusting oneself to make healthy, appropriate lifestyle changes.

Bonding — is genuine when one feels embraced by one's family. It is an emotional relationship that is unthreatened by its individual members being distinct in personhood. One is united by an unyielding sense of having a secure base, which serves to strengthen this enduring close affection. It is an emotional connection fortified by ongoing and dependable mutual respect, cooperative intent, honest communication, and complementary professional attitudes and goals.

Boundaries — invisible end points in a relationship. This line of demarcation, when crossed, sends a message to the other individual in the twosome relationship that he or she is not important. When boundaries blur, the heart of the relationship is soiled. The individual whose boundaries are violated feels disrespected, trust is tarnished, and genuine connectedness is not possible.

Burden — reflects an emotionally punishing and tiresome obligation in which the stress on both mind and body far outweighs the advantages of being a participant in the family unit.

Coalition — a temporary alliance with a third individual (an individual perceived to be both influential and supportive) for the purpose of giving aid in reassigning the "ratio of power" to the twosome system. As such, the alliance is a line of defense used by one member of the twosome system for leverage in his or her struggle to reposition and expand his or her own influence and control in the dyad.

Completion — a state of fulfillment and closure as one has aspired and obtained all that one desires, both within one's own reach and possibly beyond one's perceived reach.

Configuration — denotes the family members (each being a part of the emotional system of the family unit) as having been arranged to function and to relate in a particular way, to co-operate. In an open relationship configuration, family members are invited to embrace the journey of working toward individuation, not to fear it. In a closed relationship configuration, taking on the responsibility of defining oneself as separate from the family is an intimidating task, as it signifies a risk of challenging the rules of the family system.

Conformists — those who engage in conformity. One of two distinct influence styles in a closed relationship configuration, in which individuals seek recognition through conforming as a means of obtaining acknowledgment. When one is a conformist, one is submissive, obedient, and compliant. When one conforms, one gives the impression of being amenable or open to influence or advice. Actions get recognition through standing out and being labeled as one who is open and holds an unresistant attitude. In actuality, the conformist has learned to repress feelings and conquer the impelling inclination to oppose.

Connectedness — to function in enhancing ways as a family, both within the family's private world and within the family's public world. It is having an emotional bond born out of investing trust in another. Through that other's trustworthiness comes a feeling of safety. This act of connecting is a direct result of family members embracing the journey of individuation, while upholding the principles behind professional interdependence.

Co-operate — signifies the intent of a family-run business. The prefix "co" means together, jointly associated in action; "operate" means to perform a function, to exert power or influence, to bring about. A traditional family-run business is a system comprised of individuals joined together to collectively exert their individual powers in order to perform a function to bring about a desired effect.

Dependent One — one who forms a reputation as overly weak, overly irresponsible, overly self-indulgent, or overly out-of-control. These patterns of behavior are part of a reciprocal dependency with the Enabler, who forms a reputation as overly competent, overly dependable, overly available, or overly controlled. The cycle of this alliance repeats itself unless an intervention ensues. It is detrimental for all participants to continue in these roles as the healthiness of the family in business is held at bay.

Differentiation — having a relationship with oneself, a self that possesses characteristics that distinguish the individual from his or her family. In a healthily functioning family, one is encouraged to develop different characteristics, to be distinct in personhood, and to be emotionally mature.

Discouragement — an attitude with regard to one's own value as a person. It is in evidence when one lacks courage and confidence to risk initiating life tasks, and it represents a personal deprivation. One is not able to truly test, define, and own one's personal strengths and abilities.

Displaced loyalty — reflects susceptibility and sensitivity to falsely supporting the feelings and interests of another at the expense of being true to oneself.

Dominant figure — exerting marked influence in a social hierarchy, selectively employed as needed, and effectively overseeing and guiding learning and growth. It is a privilege to be entrusted with the position of being a dominant figure. To have credibility as a dominant figure is much more than having the power of authority. One's actions directly influence others' perceptions, such that one's behavior will either acquire students or repel students.

Dual relationship — when one plays two parts simultaneously, requiring the capacity to portray complex qualities in one's personality, both as a relative of the family and as an employee of the company. This twofold nature of being a member in a family and then transferring that membership into employment in the family business forms an alliance that is supposedly entered into for mutual benefit.

Enabler — one who forms a reputation as overly competent, overly dependable, overly available, or overly controlled. These patterns of behavior are part of a reciprocal dependency with the Dependent One, who forms a reputation as overly weak, overly irresponsible, overly self-indulgent, or overly out-of-control. The cycle of this alliance repeats itself unless an intervention ensues. It is detrimental for all participants to continue in these roles as the healthiness of the family in business is held at bay.

Entitlement — comprised of two divergent issues: (a) seeing oneself as having the right or having the grounds to seek or claim something. This issue aligns with one's defense tactics for control, manipulation, and dependency. This is an attitudinal and behavioral dynamic and a predictor of certain dilemmas that a family business may face. It is a self-serving orientation in evidence with such attitudes as *the right to control the power* or *the right to claim a position in the business* by virtue of relationship status rather than by ability and dependability. This issue hints at weaknesses in accountability and how susceptible the business is to eroding. The healthy alternative is (b) those rights of conduct that are in accordance with a standard of operation that everyone concerned finds agreeable, both on a personal level and on a social level.

Expectation — a psychological contract between family members that is comprised of an attitude exchanged between individuals or the attitude of one toward self or others with regard to future emotional profit and perceiving the probability that a desired outcome will occur. When expectations are unrealistic, anger and resentment build, which in turn invites an erosion of co-operation. It is collective unrealistic expectations that, when brought together, form a family or family-run business that is functioning devoid of psychological health.

Family busy-ness — the motivation to be in a constant state of motion, to be active. While goal-oriented, goals are not clearly defined. To be "busy" (in motion), one is in a state of "doing," but not necessarily with the goal of achieving. To be "busy" does not involve movement toward actualizing potential; rather, motivation is to undertake activities that will self-protect. Being in a state of busy-ness eliminates risk-worthy behaviors that lead to long term gratification and is accompanied by conflicted feelings, such as discouragement and guilt.

Family-run business — (defined with ideal considerations) embodies an appealing occupational environment where abundant and favorable circumstances reside for adult-to-adult skill building (not parent-to-child or husband-to-wife or sibling-to-sibling) and for the exploration of creative functioning as a cooperative and dynamic organization. As the participating family members absorb, affirm, accomplish, and embrace, so too do they capture the essence of the glorification that comes with collective winning.

Functional strength — characterized by a durable nature. It is reflected in one who has stamina to effectively endure the demands of a system that yearns to undergo a meaningful experience, in spite of the pains that come with growing emotionally.

Governing processes — the act of directing the making and administering of policy to serve as a precedent over the performance of functions in a family-run business. This process of setting and maintaining standards keeps a smooth course of operation for the good of the individual and of the whole. These standards represent a deciding influence over any emotional reactiveness that would impede the psychological and social growth of the business and its work force.

Guilt — a feeling of inadequacy as one perceives oneself as having committed an offense whereby one's conduct violated "The Family's Rules"—one's imposed value system. Or, a feeling of remorse for engaging in conduct that has violated one's own moral code. Perceiving one's conduct to be morally wrong may in fact be erroneous. One's actions may not be an actual offense, but an imagined violation influenced by accepting a value system that is not harmoniously associated with one's own self-definition, which includes behavioral limits.

Kin-Synergy — building a foundation of genuine togethering, nurtured through the self-confidence that comes from one's own internal competence in conjunction with the encouragement, support, and co-operation of others. The focal points of a family-run business' internal standards are: (a) the need to be firmly rooted in the blending of healthy self-identity with the freedom to be connected; (b) the need for all to be internally self-defined, acting upon those values associated with one's own self-definition; and (c) the need to experience unifying business objectives which yield a power far beyond that which each individual could achieve separately.

Manipulation — a means of controlling another through unfair practices to ultimately serve the manipulator's advantage. When one manipulates, he or she holds the other (the object of the manipulative scheme) in disrespect and low esteem with intent to emotionally profit by playing upon the vulnerabilities of his or her prey. It is the means by which one lures another into a compromising position through the employment of covert or overt actions.

Oppositionists — those who engage in opposition. One of two distinct influence styles in a closed relationship configuration, in which individuals seek recognition through oppositional behavior as a means of standing out. When one is an oppositionist, one is motivated to violate, to antagonize, and to combat. Oppositional behavior is a misguided attempt at differentiation, creating a way to be (not to feel) in control when one is in conflict over exploring one's role in the "adult" world of working in a family-run business. Oppositional behavior, when acted out in the workplace, causes the intensity of the family's emotional tension to heighten.

Other-defined success — an authority figure's use of power (either through another's obedience or through emulation) to impose predetermined, oftentimes ill-conceived and unrealistic, expectations onto someone else of what that person should aspire to achieve.

246

Parentified role — an inverted relationship of looking to one's business to fulfill one's unmet emotional needs and unrealistic expectations. This occurs when individuals in a family-run business, through collective emotional underdevelopment, have emotionally functioned more as children than as adults. In acting out unresolved family issues, no one has assumed the adult roles necessary to parent the family-run business. With maturity and collaborative effectiveness compromised, the business gets placed in a "parentified" role. It is an unsturdy and therefore unreliable foundation designated to influence and preserve family contacts.

Pro-social behavior — to achieve professionally as a family, one is required to learn behavior that is responsive to aligning the personal with the professional through a style of functioning that is characteristic of: (a) standards of practice that depict collaboration; (b) interventions that are effective by demonstrating power through recognition of professional procedure and conduct; and (c) voluntarily amending roles when warranted to generate and accelerate the prosperous development of "growing emotionally" as a family. When a family is rightfully concerned with the performance of its principal players, it places a value on defining professional competence and aligning it with social competence.

Psychological well-being — encompasses the thoughts and feelings that are going on within individual family members, as well as those that are exchanged between family members, as each member functions in the family-run business. These collective feelings will be reflected in the emotional overtones emanating within the system's environment. The quality of the relationship between family members takes into account: (a) the ability to be trusting and trustworthy for each other; (b) one's willingness to risk involvement, to self-disclose; (c) the emotional safety of being able to show one's professional strengths, as well as one's professional weaknesses; and (d) the encouragement and confidence to show initiative and seek professional development.

Recognition hunger — coined by Eric Berne, this term refers to an individual's psychological need for approval, a striving for social meaning.

Resilience — an inner power or emotional flexibility to recover from the misfortunes of having participated in a disordered family or a disordered family-run business environment. It is giving oneself permission to dismantle the aftereffects of destructive energies—negatives that have diminished the ability to effectively serve both the personal and professional components that make up a family-run business. Being resilient is empowering. Resilience is a function of mental health.

Resistance — an internalized code to indicate potential peril—one's personal distress call. To respond with resistance is empowering. In its dominant state, this avenue for seeking power, while protecting oneself from feeling psychologically endangered, also deprives one of optimism and enthusiasm, as well as discourages compliance. Resistance is provocative, as it thwarts co-operation. This state of unrest is unsuitable to the demands of the work environment, since it covers up feelings, stirs up disagreement, gives rise to anger, produces opposition, and creates impasses. Thus, resistance holds promise to a secondary gain—an unconscious wish to avoid change.

Rivalry — competing against a family member at the cost of that member's professional image. It is the act of measuring one's success in relation to one's perceptions of the failings of another. This antagonistic behavior undermines not only cooperative intent, but ultimately team-building.

Rules of conduct — (in regard to the occupational process) a pattern of relating or a style of interaction which includes three major measurements: work patterns, attendance, and on-the-job behavior. These measurements provide a realistic and attainable work performance guideline for addressing observable characteristics of job decline that are measurable and specific. Rigid rules and obligations generate unrealistic expectations about self and others. These rigid rules of conduct condition one to perceive oneself, one's interactions with others, and one's walk through life with a distorted outlook; efforts are evaluated by all-or-nothing thinking. One's pattern of attachment will cause one to adapt one's own rules of conduct to the family-run business work environment. These rules influence one's capacity and willingness to show cooperative intentions.

Self-identity — a psychological separateness from others that shifts focus from seeing oneself as inseparable from family to obtaining a sense that one does not have to rely upon the family for a sense of self. To be psychologically mature, one must go through a process of being able to internalize what is in one's own best interest—a self-defining act.

Self-neglect — characterized by a careless indifference to the establishment of educational, vocational, or avocational goals, as well as being inattentive to the discipline needed to fulfill said goals. In this context, it is an unfaithfulness to oneself by not making an attempt to achieve self-defined success. Although self-sabotaging, it becomes enticing to follow a path of success that is other-defined.

Social well-being — determined by the family's set of values, these social contracts are the patterns of behavior which are intended to be mutually beneficial and take into account: (a) negotiating the use of power and authority; (b) exercising cooperative intentions; and (c) defining conflicts in ways that bring enrichment to the environment through constructive resolution.

Succession planning — handing down one's esteemed business reputation from one generation to another. This transfer of authority, this shift of responsibility, is a three-fold process which involves preparing for change, implementing change, and ultimately managing change. There is an interplay between "change" and "stability" for successful succession planning to occur. One needs to be able to hand over a leadership position in a nondisruptive fashion, so that the business continues to run smoothly despite internal changes.

Time competence — the ability to function in the here-and-now and yet effectively intertwine the family's and the family-run business' past with visions and goals for its future. This is a necessary element for attaining and maintaining psychological and social well-being in the family-run business.

Togethering — feeling emotionally complete, not only within oneself, but also with significant others. This incorporates two concepts of psychological and social maturity: (a) being in possession of a healthy self-identity, in which one consciously recognizes one's own value; and (b) feeling that one is being recognized, validated for one's selfhood, and seen as a welcomed and cherished family member.

Triangular relationships — the joining together of two people in a twosome system with a distinct third person—an individual perceived to be both influential and supportive. Since all triangles are motivated by a need to gain power and influence and a need to avoid loss, this third party is selected because he or she supposedly possesses the ability to supply what the one seeking to persuade lacks, and at the same time, shares a mutual dependence. Given this perspective, triangular relationships provoke feelings and behaviors in others that direct attention away from forming a cohesive work environment.

INDEX

ABOUT THE AUTHOR

Laurie Pickàrd (pronounced Pic-card) has been contributing to the field of psychotherapy and psychoeducation since 1984, the year she received her masters degree in community counseling. As a current resident of Arizona, Laurie is state certified with the Arizona Board of Behavioral Health Examiners as a Certified Professional Counselor. Laurie is also nationally certified with the National Board of Certified Counselors, for which she is a Nationally Certified Counselor, as well as having an additional specialty with the National Board as a Masters Addiction Counselor. In addition, she is a Certified Diplomate of the American Psychotherapy Association.

In 1986, Laurie entered into supervisory training with government, private, and public sectors of Florida business. A significant proportion of her clinical work was centered on individuals (both management and non-management) seeking guidance for work-related concerns. Laurie's shift in focus, with emphasis being given to the family-run business, was a natural evolution. She has been personally connected to the world of family-run business from childhood through her adult years. From her personal and professional experiences, a philosophy and methodology was born.

A psychotherapist by profession, Laurie primarily sees herself as a change-agent, an educator. Applying her cross-utilization of skills in both counseling and business management, Laurie is a champion for those whose personal and professional quest is to be broad-minded, flexible, and knowledgeable about how to specify, refine, and appropriately implement business-life tools. This sophisticated understanding serves to strengthen psychological and social foundations. As the Director of Family Business Lifestylings, L.L.C., Laurie is dedicated, through her writings, seminars, and consulting, to guiding family-run businesses in exploring alternative and healthy ways of working together. She believes that all participants deserve to have an environmental business-life that enables them to feel encouraged, inspired, and fulfilled.

You can contact Laurie to inquire about consulting, seminars, and speaking engagements at:

Family Business Lifestylings, L.L.C.
P.O. Box 1548
Scottsdale, AZ 85252-1548
Phone: (480) 990-4436
Fax: (480) 314-3364
e-mail: info@familybusinesslife.com
web site: www.familybusinesslife.com

ORDERING INSTRUCTIONS

- Call us toll free at (877) 289-6997 or locally at (480) 481-6997, 24 hours a day, Monday through Sunday.

- Write us at Avant-Courier Press
        P.O. Box 1548
        Scottsdale, AZ 85252-1548

- Fax us at (480) 314-3364

- E-mail us at info@familybusinesslife.com

Shipping Information:
Orders must be prepaid by check, money order, VISA or MasterCard, or accompanied by an official purchase order number (pending credit approval). Please include all charges: book(s), sales tax (Arizona residents only), and shipping (see chart below).

Shipping & Handling for U.S. Orders:
Up to $20.00......................................$4.00
$20.01 to $30.00..............................$5.00
$30.01 to $60.00..............................$7.00
$60.01 to $90.00............................$10.00
$90.01 to $120.00..........................$12.00
Over $120.00........Add 10% after discount
*Shipping Carrier: We ship orders by UPS or RPS.
A $15.00 handling fee will be added to any Rush Orders.

Foreign Orders:
All foreign orders must be prepaid in U.S. funds. Call us at our toll free number for the international shipping costs specific to your location.

Discounts for Individuals, Schools, Libraries, Groups, and Associations:
Less than 5 books..................No Discount
6 to 19 books.......................10% Discount
20 or more books.................20% Discount

School Examination/Inspection Copies:

Examination copies are available on special terms to instructors wishing to consider titles for course adoption. For examination copies of titles with a list price of $20.00 and under, enclose $5.00 for postage and handling for each title requested. For titles with a list price over $20.00, enclose $8.00 for each title. An instructor may receive a maximum of 4 examination copies per year. Please make requests on school letterhead, citing course and enrollment. Shipment will be made only to a school address.

School Desk Copies:

Complimentary desk copies are available once a title has been adopted for a course with an enrollment of 10 or more students. It is our policy to provide a desk copy once we have received the textbook order from the instructor's college bookstore.

Discounts for Bookstores:

1 book....................................No Discount
2 to 4 books..........................20% Discount
5 to 24 books.......................30% Discount
25 to 49 books.....................40% Discount
50 to 99 books.....................43% Discount
100 to 499 books.................45% Discount
500 or more books..............50% Discount

Credit Terms (Upon Approval):

The above discounts apply only if the invoice(s) are paid within 30 days of the invoice date. After such time, a $1\frac{1}{2}\%$ finance charge will be added. We reserve the right to refuse orders from accounts that have unpaid invoices over 60 days old.

Special Note:

Dates, prices, titles, and manufacturer specifications of all books are subject to change without notice. Returns must be in resaleable condition (in original shrink-wrap), and there is a 10% restocking fee. Please call for a returns authorization prior to shipping any books back to us.

BOOK RETURN POLICY

1. Books received in damaged condition will be replaced promptly by Avant-Courier Press, provided that the damage is reported to us upon receipt. Save damaged cartons until any claim is settled, and contact Avant-Courier Press for an authorization to return merchandise.

2. Undamaged books (in original shrink-wrap) may be returned for credit up to but not more than one year after the invoice date. A 10% restocking charge will apply.

3. Payment for books must have been made in order to receive a credit.

4. Books must be in saleable condition, unsoiled, free from dealer marks or labels, in original shrink-wrap, properly packed, and shipped prepaid.

5. Credit will be issued for the amount paid (less restocking fee) if invoice information is provided. Otherwise, credit will be issued at maximum discount.

6. Credit memos are valid for one year from the date that they are issued, after which they become void.

7. Credit will be applied to the invoice on which books were purchased. Deductions by the customer must reference our Invoice Number or the customer's Purchase Order Number.

8. No trade title will be accepted for return beyond three months after being declared out-of-print.

9. Any returns that do not meet the above criteria will be sent back at the customer's expense.

10. All claims of non-receipt must be made within 60 days of the date of invoice or they will not be honored.

Returns Address:

Avant-Courier Press

14795 N. 78th Way #300
Scottsdale, AZ 85260
Toll Free Phone: (877) 289-6997
Local Phone: (480) 481-6997
Fax: (480) 314-3364